AF386724

THE BIG BOOK OF CARS

ROB COLSON

WAYLAND

Are you ready for a wild ride through the world of cars? There's a lot to explore ...

RACING CARS

Where better to start exploring the thrilling world of cars, than with the speed and power of racing machines? Meet the cars built for speed and victory on the racetrack …

A SHORT HISTORY OF SOME MOTOR RACING FIRSTS

EVENT	LOCATION	YEAR	WINNER	CAR
First official organised race	Paris to Rouen, France	1894	Albert Lemaître (France)	Peugeot Type 7
First Indy 500	Indianapolis, USA	1911	Ray Harroun (USA)	Marmon Wasp
First 24 Hours of Le Mans	Le Mans, France	1923	André Lagache, René Léonard (France)	Chenard-Walcker Type U3
First Monaco Grand Prix	Monte Carlo, Monaco	1929	William Grover-Williams (UK)	Bugatti T35B
First NASCAR race	Charlotte Fairgrounds Speedway, USA	1949	Jim Roper (USA)	Lincoln Cosmopolitan
First Formula 1 Grand Prix	Silverstone, England	1950	Giuseppe Farina (Italy)	Alfa Romeo 158
First Official National Hot Rod Association drag race	Great Bend, Kansas	1955	Calvin Rice (USA)	Custom drag racer

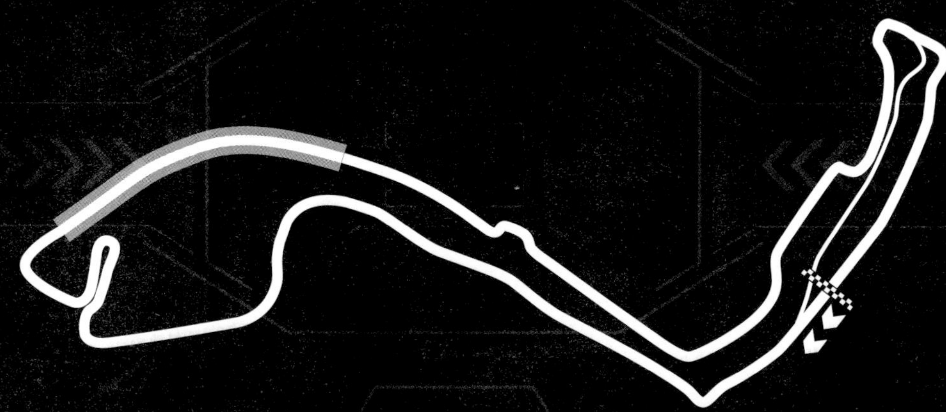

MOTOR RACING

Ever since the motor car was invented in the 1880s, people have raced cars. The earliest motor races were events run by enthusiastic amateurs, who competed in their own cars. Later, manufacturers developed new kinds of racing car, pushing the limits of technology.

Cars line up on the grid for the 1934 French Grand Prix at the Autodrome de Linas-Montlhèry circuit, near Paris.

FIRST RACE

The first organised motor race was held in France in 1894. Twenty-one cars competed in the race, which took place over a 126-km course from Paris to Rouen in France. The winner, a Peugeot driven by Frenchman Albert Lemaître, completed the course in just under 7 hours.

In their design, early cars resembled the carriages pulled by horses. They were fitted with engines that generated 3 hp (**horsepower**), meaning that it would take three horses to pull the carriage with the same power.

The first cars had a top speed of about 20 km/h.

THE BIG PRIZE

By the early 20th century, races known as Grand Prix (French for 'Big Prize') were being held. Cars raced around circuits formed from public roads or on purpose-built tracks. In the 1930s, new racing cars were developed specially for Grand Prix races. The fastest could reach top speeds of more than 400 km/h.

ROUND THE WORLD

The longest motor race in history took place in 1908. Six cars lined up for the start of the race in New York on the east coast of the USA. They drove across the USA to San Francisco, up to Seattle, from there to Japan by steamer boat, to Siberia by ship and then through Asia and Europe to Paris. Three cars completed the race, driving a total of 16,700 km in just under six months of racing.

Competitors line up for the start of the 1908 round the world race.

RACING FOR ALL

American autocross is a form of racing that allows anybody with a car to compete. Instead of driving against each other, competitors complete timed laps of the course, which is marked out with traffic cones. There are various classes for different kinds of car.

This Chevrolet Corvette Stingray is competing in an autocross class for powerful muscle cars.

CLASSIC F1
MASERATI 250F

Formula 1 (F1) is the ultimate racing competition, with races held across the world. Beginning in 1950, the first decade was dominated by Italian cars. The Maserati 250F raced between 1954 and 1958.

MASERATI 250F

WEIGHT:
670 kg

ENGINE:
2.5 litre, 6 cylinders

POWER:
240 hp

TRANSMISSION:
5-speed

TOP SPEED:
290 km/h

SIMPLE DESIGN

F1 cars in the 1950s looked very different from today's high-tech machines. With its simple tube-shaped **chassis** and open cabin, the Maserati 250F offered little protection to the driver. It took a lot of courage to take it up to full speed at nearly 300 km/h. Crashes were frequent, and 15 drivers were killed in the first decade of F1 racing.

FAMOUS VICTORY

Legendary Argentinian driver Juan Manuel Fangio won five F1 titles in the 1950s. He won his last title in 1957 in a Maserati 250F. Fangio's final win came in the German Grand Prix at the Nürburgring circuit. Finding himself 50 seconds behind the leader after a pit stop had gone wrong, Fangio stormed to victory, breaking the lap record 10 times to take the lead on the final lap.

Fangio (see right) on his way to victory at the 1957 German Grand Prix.

FRONT ENGINE LAYOUT

*The 2.5-litre engine sat at the front of the 250F. From 1959 onwards, new F1 cars placed the engine behind the driver, which gave the cars better balance, making them easier to **handle**. The Maserati 250F found itself outpaced by these mid-engine cars, and by 1961, all drivers had switched over to the new design.*

MERCEDES-AMG F1 W10

Racing on tricky courses with sharp turns, F1 cars are designed to take corners at breathtaking speed. Each year, the cars must meet strict new rules regarding engine size, body shape, fuel capacity and safety features. The Mercedes-AMG F1 W10 won both the Constructors' and Drivers' Championships in 2019.

*The engine sits behind the driver, covered by the **aerodynamic** body.*

The wings are tilted at an angle to produce enough downforce but not too much drag.

DOWNFORCE

To take corners at high speed without skidding, F1 cars need to create lots of downforce. Most of this is generated by the front and rear wings. As air passes over the wings, it presses down on them, helping the tyres to grip the track when taking corners. However, this also increases the force of **drag**, which slows the cars down. On fast tracks, wing size is reduced to increase speed on the long straights.

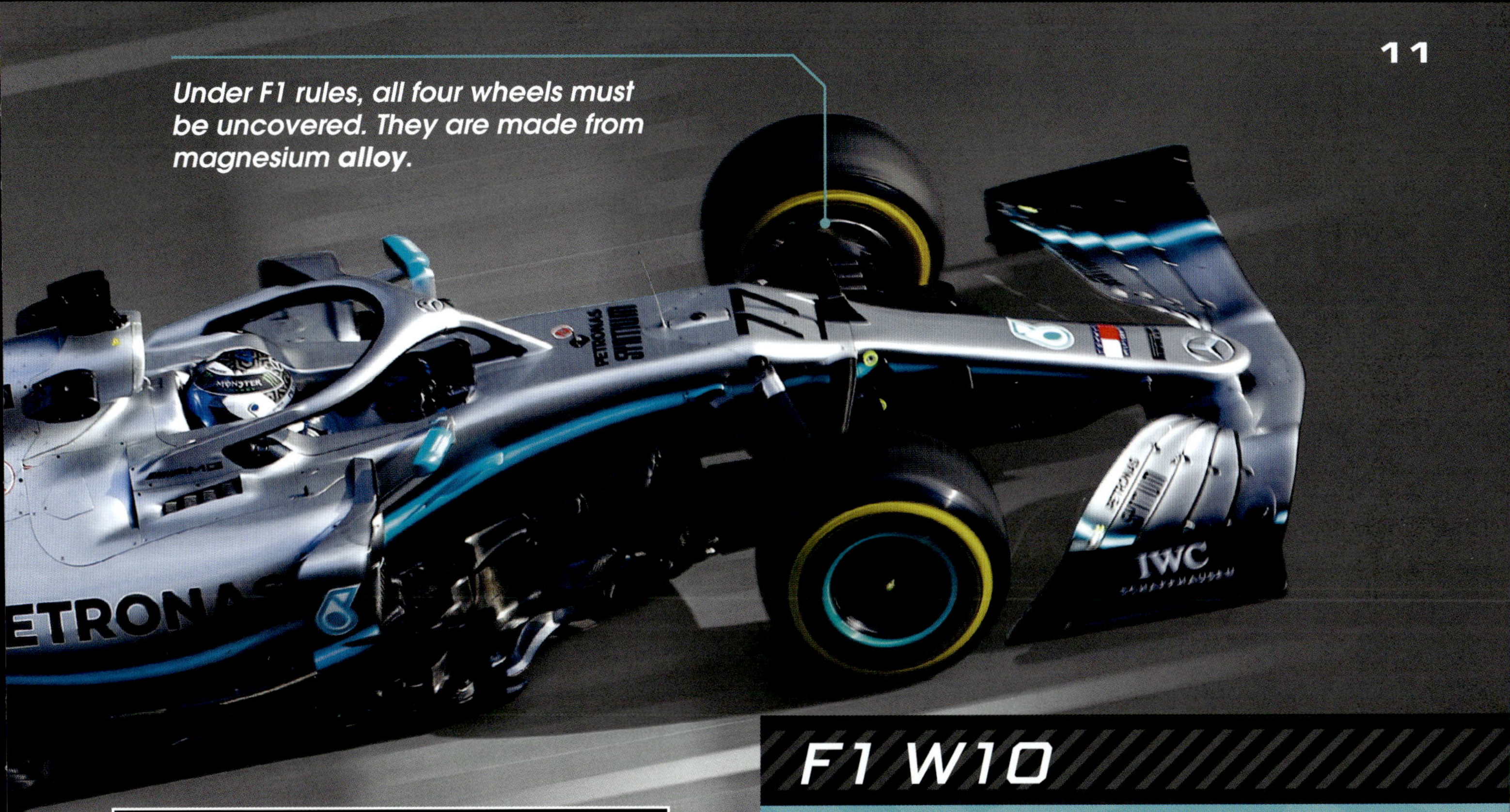

TECH POINT

A T-shaped 'halo' wraps around the open cockpit just above the level of the driver's helmet, protecting the head in the event of a crash. The halo is now a compulsory part of all F1 cars. It must be able to withstand a weight of more than 12 tonnes. Made from lightweight titanium, the halo weighs about 9 kg. Manufacturers experiment with its shape to make the halo as aerodynamic as possible.

F1 W10

WEIGHT:
743 kg

0 – 100 KM/H:
2.1 seconds

ENGINE:
1.6 litre, 6 cylinders

TOP SPEED:
352 km/h

CONTROL CONSOLE

The steering wheel is also the driver's control console, allowing them to perform every function without taking their hands from the wheel. It has 25 buttons and switches, controlling gear changes, brake settings, power adjustors and communications with the pit lane. On a typical lap of a race circuit, which is about 4 km long, the driver will change gear about 50 times.

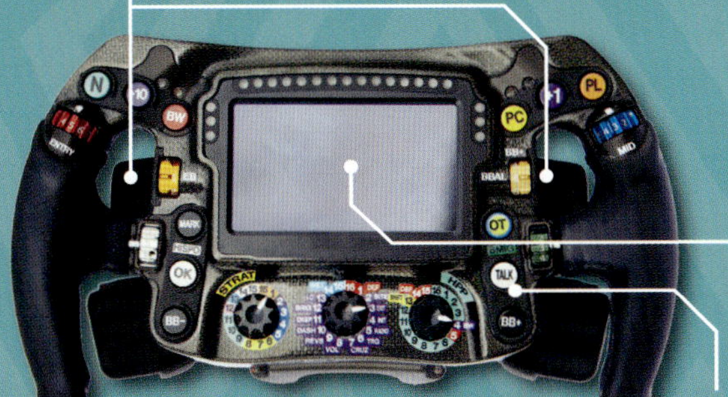

DALLARA DW12

IndyCar is the premier open-wheel car racing championship in the US. This annual series is named after its most famous race, the Indianapolis 500, known as the Indy 500. '500' refers to the race length of 500 miles (805 km). All teams use the same DW12 chassis, made by Italian manufacturer Dallara.

AERODYNAMICS

An aero kit is fitted around the chassis of the car. This is made up of lots of adjustable parts designed to produce downforce to keep the cars on the road when cornering, while also allowing them to cut through the air along high-speed straights. The parts can all be adjusted to suit each of the 17 circuits in the IndyCar season, which are a mix of tight, winding tracks and high-speed ovals.

WINGS
These provide downforce.

TECH POINT

The core of the Dallara chassis is designed for maximum driver safety. The driver sits inside a safety cell, surrounded by energy-absorbing foam. Drivers also wear a HANS (Head And Neck Support) device, which prevents skull fractures in high-speed accidents.

As all drivers use the same chassis, IndyCar races are a test of pure driving ability and the races are closely fought.

ENGINE COWLING
This is a slick, aerodynamic cover for the engine.

SIDEPODS
These protect the sides of the car. They also help to cool the engine, provide an aerodynamic shape and protect the driver in case of a side impact.

DW12

ENGINE:
2.2 litre, 6 cylinders

WEIGHT:
741 kg

POWER:
650 hp (speedways),
700 hp (road courses)

TOP SPEED:
386 km/h

0–100 KM/H:
3.0 seconds

ENGINE AND FUEL:
The cars are fitted with standard engines, supplied either by Chevrolet or Honda. The fuel capacity is limited to 70 litres, which makes the refuelling strategy a vital part of a race. During the Indy 500, cars need to refuel at least six times.

TOYOTA TS050

In endurance races, cars complete as many laps as possible over a fixed time period. They include separate classes of cars racing at the same time: Le Mans Prototypes (LMPs), made just for endurance racing; and Grand Tourers, which are modified road cars. The Toyota TS050 Hybrid was a revolutionary car featuring a combined petrol engine and electric. It raced between 2016 and 2020.

The engine and battery were behind the driver.

RACING RULES

With their wide, low chassis, large rear wings and roaring engines, LMP cars are unmistakable on the track. Unlike open-wheel cars such as F1 cars, racing rules require all mechanical parts to be covered by bodywork. They are aerodynamically shaped to produce maximum lap times with minimum fuel consumption, as the fuel used in a race is limited. All cars must conform to a strict set of rules and dimensions.

Toyota's two cars finished first and second in seven of the eight races in the 2018–2019 season.

The chassis featured a lightweight carbon fibre **monocoque**.

TS050

TECH POINT

The car, like its successor, the Toyota GR010 Hybrid, was **hybrid**, meaning that it was powered by a petrol engine and an electric motor. The batteries for the motor were charged by energy recovered when the car braked, giving the driver the option to add extra power when needed. To add even more power, the engine had a twin-turbo. Turbo chargers reuse energy from the exhaust. The exhaust fumes are forced down a narrow tube, where they spin a **turbine**. The turbine is linked to a compressor, which sucks air into the engine, helping the fuel to burn.

ENGINE:
2.4 litre, 6 cylinders

WEIGHT:
895 kg

POWER:
1,000 hp

TOP SPEED ON THE TRACK:
340 km/h

0–100 KM/H:
2 seconds

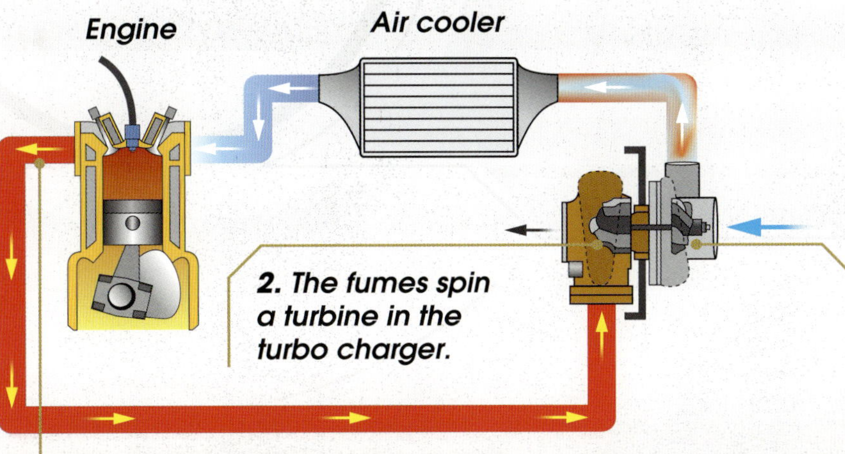

DRAGSTERS

These monsters are the biggest, fastest and noisiest racing cars of all. They have the best acceleration of any racing machine. Racing side-by-side on a straight 305-metre track, they hit the finish line in under 4 seconds, reaching speeds of more than 500 km/h. Blink and you'll miss it!

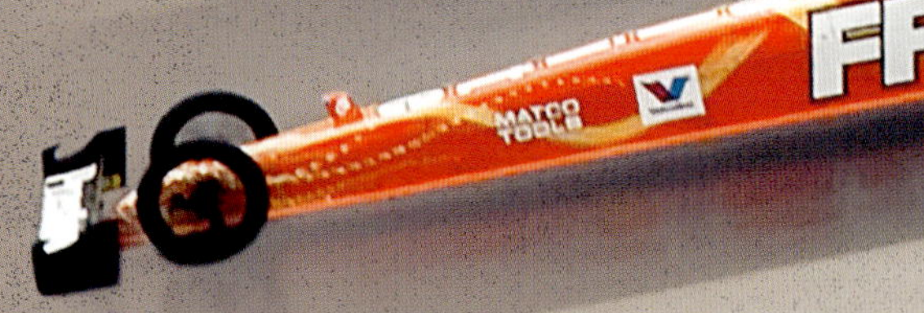

HIGH-SPEED THRILLS

Drag races, in which cars or motorbikes line up next to one another for a sprint race, have been popular ever since motor vehicles were invented. Top fuel races, with the very fastest cars, were first officially organised in the US in 1963.

At most events, cars race two at a time, but at the Four-Wide Nationals in Concord, North Carolina, there are four lanes.

BURNOUT
Before the start of the race, drivers perform a burnout. They spin the wheels on the spot, creating billowing clouds of smoke. This gets the tyres up to racing temperature. It also creates a lot of noise. A top fuel dragster is as loud as a jet plane!

TOP FUEL DRAGSTER

ENGINE:
8.2 litre, 8 cylinders

LENGTH:
up to 8 metres

POWER:
at least 11,000 hp

0–100 KM/H:
0.8 seconds

WEIGHT:
1,057 kg

RECORD SPEED:
552.26 km/h
(Brittany Force, 2025)

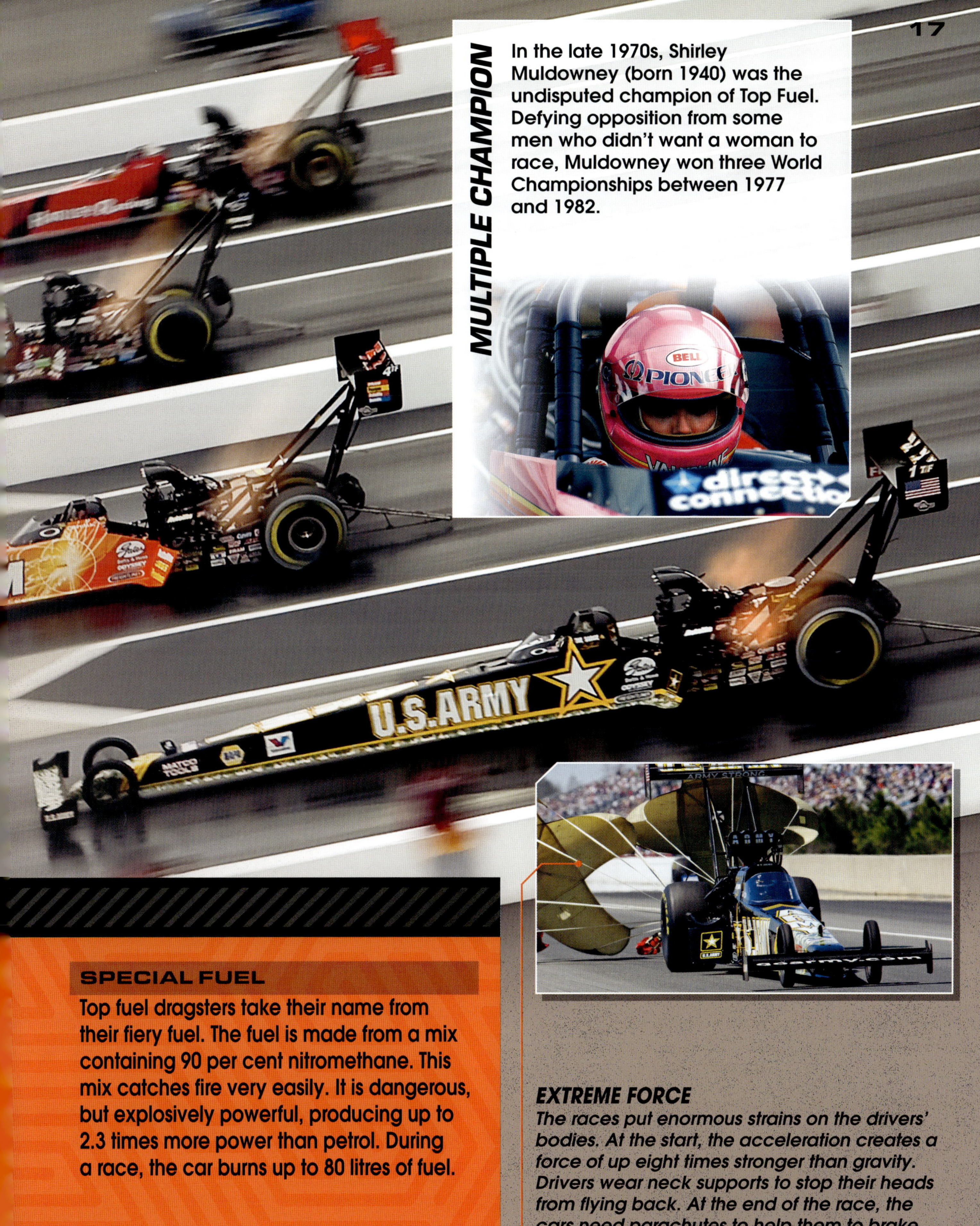

MULTIPLE CHAMPION

In the late 1970s, Shirley Muldowney (born 1940) was the undisputed champion of Top Fuel. Defying opposition from some men who didn't want a woman to race, Muldowney won three World Championships between 1977 and 1982.

SPECIAL FUEL

Top fuel dragsters take their name from their fiery fuel. The fuel is made from a mix containing 90 per cent nitromethane. This mix catches fire very easily. It is dangerous, but explosively powerful, producing up to 2.3 times more power than petrol. During a race, the car burns up to 80 litres of fuel.

EXTREME FORCE

The races put enormous strains on the drivers' bodies. At the start, the acceleration creates a force of up eight times stronger than gravity. Drivers wear neck supports to stop their heads from flying back. At the end of the race, the cars need parachutes to help them to brake.

CHEVROLET CAMARO ZL1

Stock car races are competitions for ordinary road cars that have been modified for the track. The biggest stock car competition in the world is the NASCAR Cup Series, which is contested in a series of 36 races held across the USA.

CHAMPION MODEL

Chevrolet are the most successful manufacturer in the NASCAR Cup Series. Their current car is the Camaro ZL1. While it looks like the ordinary production model from the outside, the NASCAR version has been built very differently.

OVAL SPEEDWAY
Most NASCAR races are held on oval speedways such as the Charlotte Motor Speedway, with banked corners that allow the cars to maintain hair-raising speeds for the whole race.

The first part of a stock car to be built is the **roll cage**. This is made of thick metal tubing and it protects the driver in a crash. The body is built around the roll cage using handmade metal panels. These are shaped to make the car as aerodynamic as possible, as it will need to maintain speeds over 300 km/h on the fast oval tracks.

CAMARO ZL1

DURABLE ENGINE

The engine is specially designed for racing, with durable parts that can withstand high temperatures and pressures. The engine needs to cope with 6,400 rpm at times, and it is tested thoroughly before it is fitted to the car.

ENGINE:
5.86 litre, 8 cylinders

TOP POWER:
750 hp

WEIGHT:
1,500 kg

The tyres are filled with pure nitrogen instead of air. This is done to minimise moisture inside the tyre, which can cause unwanted increases in pressure at high temperatures.

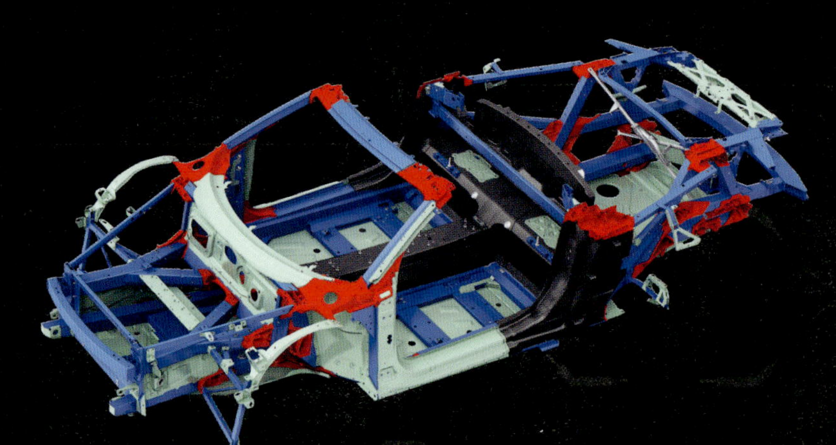

SPORTS CARS

It's time to cruise into the sleek world of sports cars – stylish machines that make every drive feel like an adventure!

SPORTS CARS THAT MADE HISTORY

YEAR	MODEL	MANUFACTURER	COUNTRY	TOP SPEED	SPORTS CAR FIRST
1903	Simplex 60hp	Mercedes	Germany	109 km/h	First production car made for speed
1923	Type-U3	Chennard-Walcker	France	120 km/h	Won the first Le Mans 24 Hour endurance race
1949	XK120	Jaguar	UK	200 km/h	First production car to break the 200 km/h barrier
1951	G2	Glasspar	USA	170 km/h (approx.)	First sports car with an all-fibreglass body
1953	550 Spyder	Porsche	Germany	230 km/h	First porsche racing car, which won the first race it entered
1962	Jetfire	Oldsmobile	USA	177 km/h	First sports car to be fitted with a turbocharger
1964	NSU Wankel Spider	NSU	Germany	153 km/h	First production car with a Wankel rotary engine
1983	Ruf BTR	Ruf Automobile GmbH	Germany	305 km/h	First production car to break the 300 km/h barrier
1991	EB110	Bugatti	France	338 km/h	First sports car with a carbon-fibre monocoque chassis
2005	Veyron 16.4	Bugatti	France	407 km/h	First production car to break the 400 km/h barrier
2008	Roadster	Tesla	USA	201 km/h	First all-electric sports car
2010	Cr-Z	Honda	Japan	200 km/h	First hybrid sports car

WHAT IS A SPORTS CAR?

Sports cars are stylish vehicles made to look good and move quickly. They are usually small cars with just two seats. With sharp handling and powerful engines, they give the driver the feel of a racing car.

THE FIRST SPORTS CAR

The Mercedes 60hp was the first car to be produced for speed. Originally made in 1903, it was the fastest production car of its day, with a top speed of up to 130 km/h. The car's 60 **horsepower (hp)** was generated by a huge 9.25 litre, four-**cylinder** engine.

IMPROVING PERFORMANCE

Manufacturers are constantly seeking to improve their cars' performance. In the 1980s, **turbochargers** were added to the engines of many sports cars. These force extra air into the cylinders to increase their power. In recent years, new high-tech materials, such as **carbon fibre reinforced plastic**, have been developed to make the car bodies and **chassis** lighter and to increase speed.

The Alfa Romeo 4C is a
modern sports car with a
light carbon-fibre and
aluminium body and a
turbocharged engine.

ROAD AND TRACK

Many sports cars are
designed both for the road
and for racing on the track.
They are often stripped of
any extras to save weight.
They are also given a stiff
suspension, to improve
handling, and have parts
such as rear wings added to
improve **aerodynamics**.

STYLE ICONS

Some sports cars have become famous because of their unique, stylish
designs. The Jaguar E-Type, made from 1961 to 1975, is widely considered
to be one of the best cars ever, and is a highly desired collector's item.

*A Jaguar E-Type
Convertible*

6C 2500

Italian manufacturer Alfa Romeo created some of the best sports cars of the 1930s and 1940s. The 6C 2500 was a range of six-cylinder cars. They were famed for their reliability, and many are still running.

MANY MAKERS

Alfa Romeo designed the basic shape and engine of the 6C 2500, but it was hand-built by a number of small companies across Italy. For this reason, many slightly different versions of the car exist. All of them feature Alfa Romeo's distinctive triangular front grille.

TECH POINT

In 1948, Alfa Romeo produced a racing version of the 6C 2500 called the Competizione Berlinetta. They cut down the frame of the car to save weight and fitted it with a more powerful engine to produce a top speed of 200 km/h. Three models were built, of which just one survives today. It sold in 2024 for $3.53 million dollars.

The car was shortened by 20 mm to improve its cornering ability.

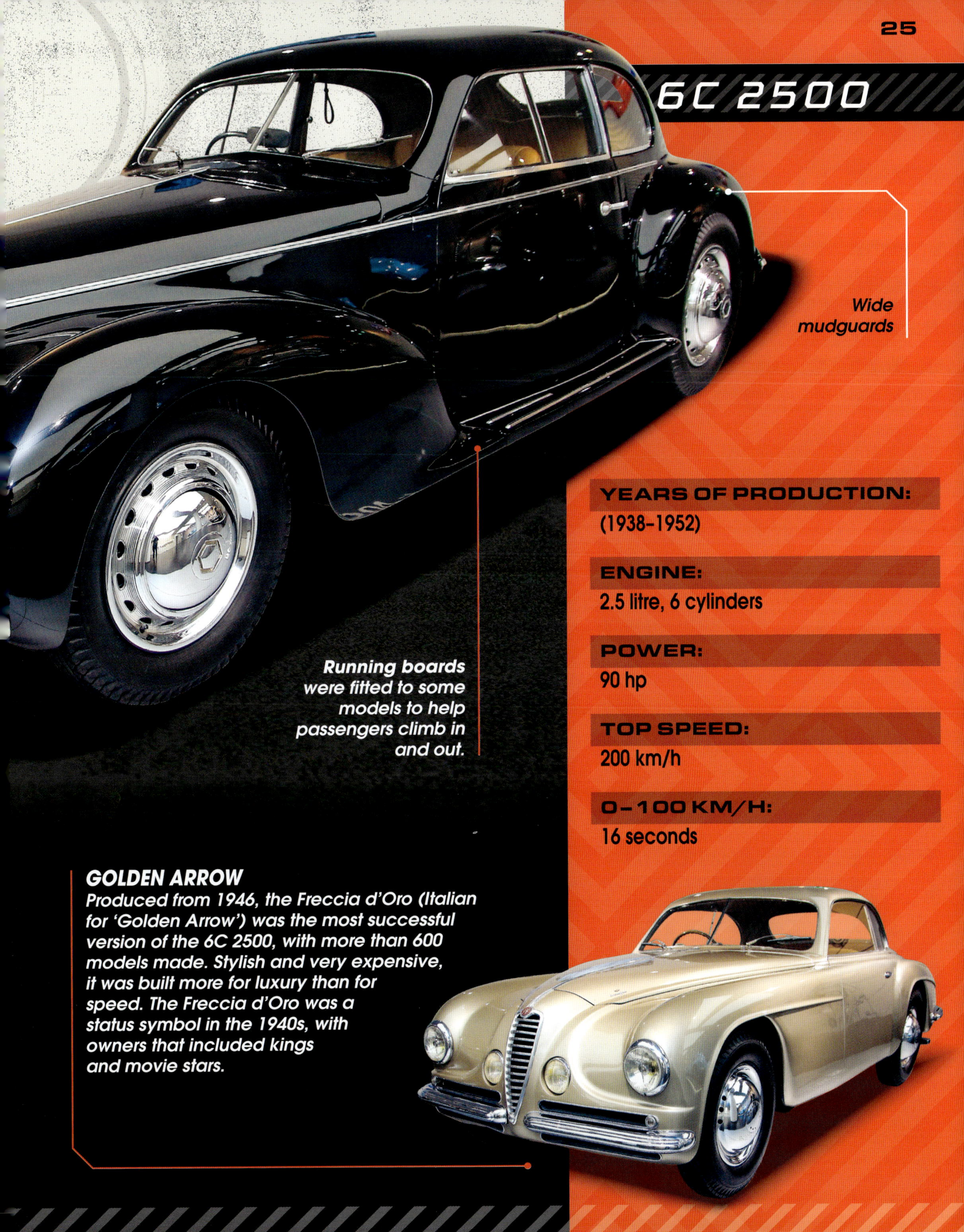

6C 2500

YEARS OF PRODUCTION:
(1938–1952)

ENGINE:
2.5 litre, 6 cylinders

POWER:
90 hp

TOP SPEED:
200 km/h

0–100 KM/H:
16 seconds

GOLDEN ARROW

Produced from 1946, the Freccia d'Oro (Italian for 'Golden Arrow') was the most successful version of the 6C 2500, with more than 600 models made. Stylish and very expensive, it was built more for luxury than for speed. The Freccia d'Oro was a status symbol in the 1940s, with owners that included kings and movie stars.

CHEVROLET
CORVETTE C1

In 1953, to compete with the stylish cars arriving in the USA from Europe, General Motors (GM) created the Chevrolet Corvette, a curvy two-seater convertible. The first generation of the Corvette, the C1, was produced until 1962.

In 1958, the car was given twin headlights and extra chrome trim, following the fashion of the day.

TECH POINT

The body of the first Corvette C1 was made from fibreglass. First developed as a building material in 1936, fibreglass is a mix of glass and plastic that is strong but lightweight. However, customers reported faults in the bodywork and disliked its rough finish.

MOUNTAIN RACE

The 1953 Corvette looked the part, but it was less powerful than its European equivalents and GM struggled to sell it. This all changed in 1955 when Chevrolet engineer, Zora Arkus-Duntov, replaced the **automatic** 6-cylinder engine with a **manual** 8-cylinder engine. This added 45 hp. Arkus-Duntov, who was also a racing driver, showcased the new model's abilities by setting a new record time for a **stock car** in the annual 'Race to the Clouds' hill climb at Pikes Peak, Colorado.

A 1955 Corvette C1

This open-top convertible sports car could be fitted with a soft or hard removable roof.

CORVETTE C1

YEARS OF PRODUCTION:
1953–1962 (first generation)

ENGINE:
From 3.9 to 5.4 litres, 8 cylinders (from 1955)

POWER:
150 hp up to 360 hp (depending on model)

TOP SPEED:
201 km/h to 231 km/h (depending on model)

0–100 KM/H:
7-11 seconds (depending on model)

MODERN CORVETTES

Modern Corvettes are built for speed and style. They use powerful V8 engines and sleek shapes tested in wind tunnels to cut through the air. Some models can go faster than 300 km/h. Each new generation adds better technology and design, making the Corvette one of the most famous sports cars in the world.

The rear wing adds downforce.

The air intakes keep the tyres cool.

911

With more than 1 million cars produced since 1963, the 911 is Porsche's most popular car and one of the most successful sports cars ever. The model has been continually updated, while maintaining the same distinctive shape.

The powerful 911 Carrera RS was made in 1973 for racing.

CREATING THE SHAPE
The 911 was developed from sketches made in 1959 by Ferdinand 'Butzi' Porsche (1935–2012, left), Butzi was the grandson of Ferdinand Porsche, the founder of the company and designer of the VW Beetle.

EIGHTH-GENERATION 911

Each new generation of 911 builds on the last. The eighth-generation 911 (left), produced in 2018, features a powerful 3-litre turbocharged engine that delivers 444 hp and a top speed of 312 km/h. It has been engineered to give better weight distribution, improving handling at high speeds.

TECH POINT

The engine of the 911 sits above the rear axle. The extra weight at the rear gives the car excellent grip when it accelerates. However, it also makes it harder to handle. Up to 1998, the engine was cooled by air, but it was prone to overheating when standing in traffic, as air could not pass through the engine. This system was replaced in 1998 by a water-cooling system, in which water is pumped through passages in the engine block.

The engine is behind the rear wheels.

911

YEARS OF PRODUCTION:
1963–1998 (air-cooled engine)

ENGINE:
2.0–3.6 litre, 6 cylinders

POWER:
130 hp (1963)

TOP SPEED:
210 km/h (1963)

0–100 KM/H:
8.7 seconds

LOTUS ESPRIT

This wedge-shaped sports car from UK manufacturer Lotus had the sharp angles that were typical of 1970s design. Small, light and extremely nimble, the Esprit was famous for its great handling.

ESPRIT

PRODUCTION:
1976–2004 (Series 1: 1976-1978)

ENGINE:
2 litre, 4 cylinders (Series 1)

POWER:
160 hp

TOP SPEED:
214 km/h

0–100 KM/H:
8 seconds

Pop-up headlights

The Maserati Boomerang concept car

'FOLDED PAPER'
The Esprit was designed by Italian Giorgetto Giugiaro (born 1938). He based its look on the Boomerang, a **concept car** he had developed for Maserati in 1971. Giugiaro's angular style became known as the 'folded paper'. He would later create similar designs for the BMW M1 and the DMC DeLorean.

The wedge-shaped design was very aerodynamic.

TECH POINT
To produce top performance, Lotus concentrated on keeping their cars as light as possible. The Esprit's lightweight fibreglass body was mounted on a tubular steel chassis. The engine was placed behind the driver, as in a racing car, to give great balance. With only four cylinders, the engine was small and light. The early models weighed just 900 kg, and it quickly gained a reputation for excellent handling, even though it lacked the power of a larger car.

BOND SUBMARINE
The Esprit featured in the 1977 Bond movie The Spy Who Loved Me *with a special 'submarine mode'. To film the Esprit transforming itself into a sub, seven different models were made.*
The final car seen in the movie was a fully operational submarine.

MAZDA
RX-7

This small Japanese sports car packed a punch in performance. The first generation sold nearly half a million models, but it is a rare sight on the roads today as its compact engine lacked durability.

SMALL BUT POWERFUL

The RX-7 was designed primarily for the home market in Japan, where large cars are taxed heavily. The tiny Wankel engine complied with Japanese tax rules while producing good power. It sat just behind the front axle, giving the car great balance, and the RX-7 became popular for its handling.

TECH POINT

Most car engines contain cylinders, inside which fuel burns to create pressure that pumps pistons up and down. In a Wankel engine, fuel is burnt to create a circular motion.
Inside an oval-shaped chamber, a three-sided rotor turns around a central shaft. On one side of the chamber, spark plugs ignite the fuel. On the other side, fuel enters through the intake, and fumes leave through the exhaust.

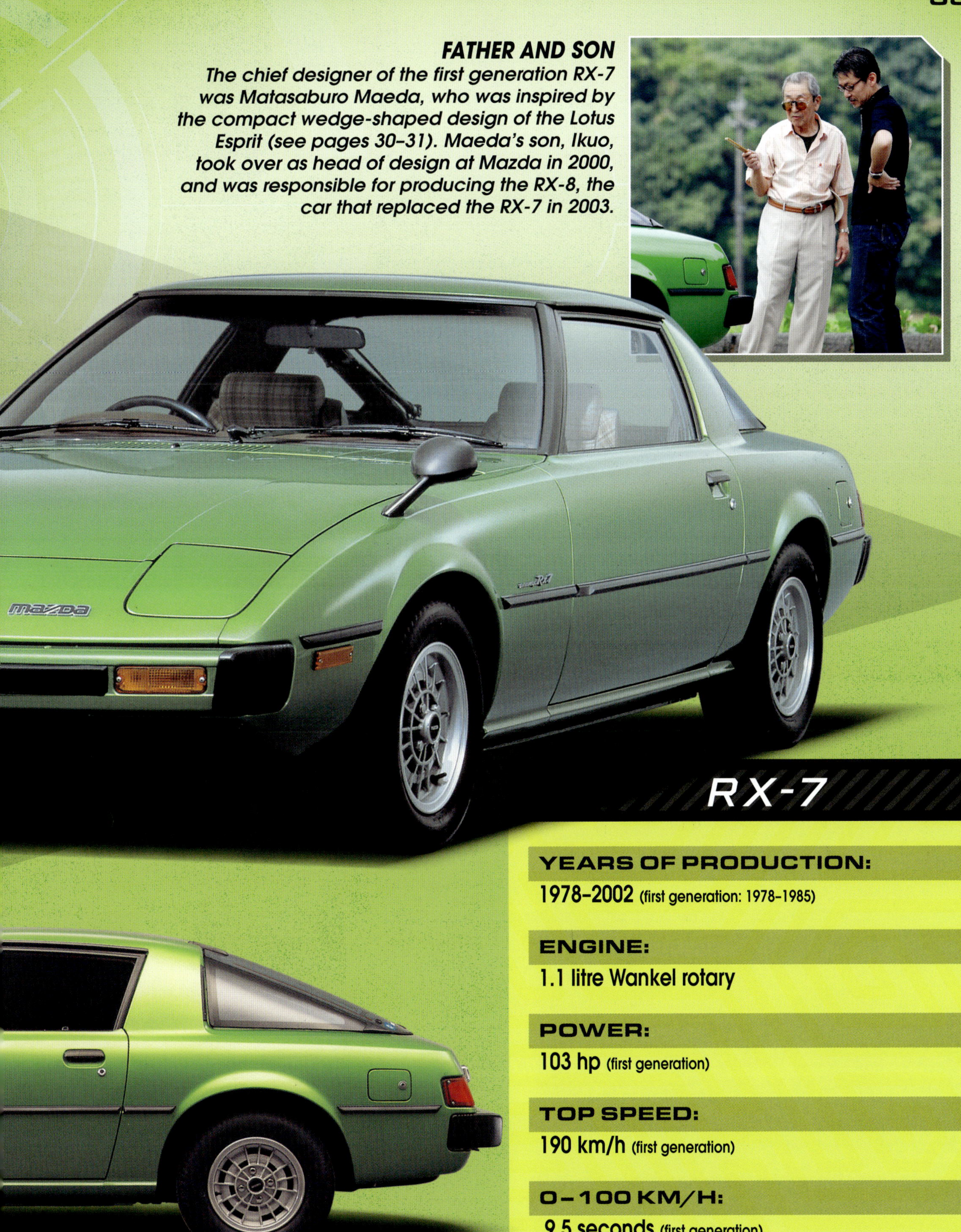

RX-7

YEARS OF PRODUCTION:

1978–2002 (first generation: 1978–1985)

ENGINE:

1.1 litre Wankel rotary

POWER:

103 hp (first generation)

TOP SPEED:

190 km/h (first generation)

0–100 KM/H:

9.5 seconds (first generation)

F40

Low, wide
and loud, the
F40 was a classic
Ferrari sports car, created by
the Italian manufacturer to mark its
40th anniversary. At the time, it was Ferrari's
most powerful, fastest and most expensive car.

BUILT FOR SPEED

To keep weight to a minimum, the F40
came with very few frills. There was no
sound system, although you would have
struggled to hear the radio over the
roaring engine. There were no carpets
or glove box, and it had only minimal
air conditioning.

To maximise power, the engine was fitted with turbochargers, which pushed extra air into the cylinders. This generated a lot of heat. To keep the engine cool, the body was shaped to allow plenty of air to pass around the engine. Wide vents either side of the car directed air over the engine, which sat behind the driver.

F40

YEARS OF PRODUCTION:
1987–1992

ENGINE:
2.9 litre, 8 cylinders

POWER:
478 hp

TOP SPEED:
324 km/h

0–100 KM/H:
4.1 seconds

RACING MODEL

Ferrari produced 19 extra-powerful models of the F40 for track racing. With an upgraded engine producing around 700 hp, the racing car had a top speed of 367 km/h. Today, these models are highly prized collectors' items. One was sold in 2019 for more than £4 million.

Twin exhaust pipes sit either side of a pipe from the turbochargers.

F-TYPE

The Jaguar F-Type was Jaguar's flagship sports car, packed with cutting-edge technology. It earned a reputation as the company's fastest model. Production ended in mid-2024, marking the end of Jaguar's petrol-powered two-seat sports cars.

IAN CALLUM

Ian Callum (born 1954) from Scotland submitted a design to Jaguar in 1968 aged just 14, in the hope it would land him a job. He joined the company 30 years later as Director of Design. Before joining Jaguar, Callum designed the DB7 and Vanquish for Aston Martin.

PROJECT 7

In 2014, Jaguar produced a limited edition of a convertible F-Type called Project 7 (right). With a 5-litre turbocharged engine, it was Jaguar's fastest-ever production car. The car was kitted out in specially developed aerodynamic parts and fitted with race-inspired bucket seats.

F-TYPE

YEARS OF PRODUCTION:
2013–2024

ENGINE:
2 litre, 4 cylinders (300PS version)

POWER:
296 hp

TOP SPEED:
250 km/h (electronically limited)

0–100 KM/H:
5.7 seconds

TECH POINT

The F-Type was made for maximum style and safety. In the event of a crash, its aluminium body has parts that are designed to crumple to reduce the force on the passengers. If the car hits a pedestrian, sensors in the bumper trigger two small airbags, which lift the bonnet by a few centimetres to soften the blow.

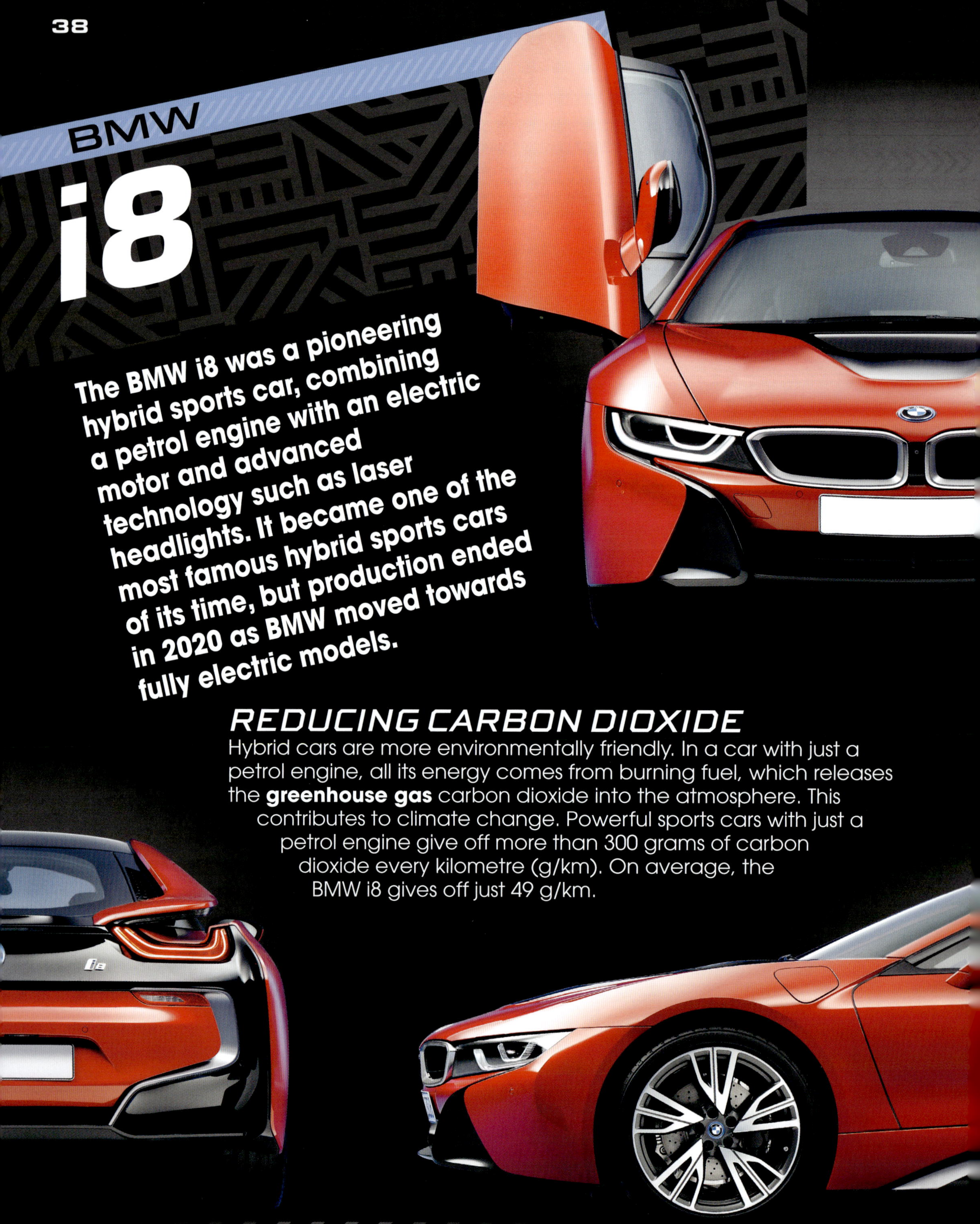

BMW i8

The BMW i8 was a pioneering hybrid sports car, combining a petrol engine with an electric motor and advanced technology such as laser headlights. It became one of the most famous hybrid sports cars of its time, but production ended in 2020 as BMW moved towards fully electric models.

REDUCING CARBON DIOXIDE

Hybrid cars are more environmentally friendly. In a car with just a petrol engine, all its energy comes from burning fuel, which releases the **greenhouse gas** carbon dioxide into the atmosphere. This contributes to climate change. Powerful sports cars with just a petrol engine give off more than 300 grams of carbon dioxide every kilometre (g/km). On average, the BMW i8 gives off just 49 g/km.

i8

The rear wheels of the i8 are powered by the engine, while the electric motor turns the front wheels, taking its energy from a battery. The battery can be charged from a power socket, and it is also charged while the car is on the move by recovering energy from the brakes. The engine, motor and battery are arranged across the car to give it perfect balance.

The 'butterfly' doors open upwards, allowing access to the car in tight spaces.

YEARS OF PRODUCTION:
2014–2020

ENGINE:
1.5 litre, 3 cylinders, plus an electric motor

POWER:
engine 228 hp; motor 141 hp

TOP SPEED:
limited to 250 km/h

0–100 KM/H:
4.4 seconds

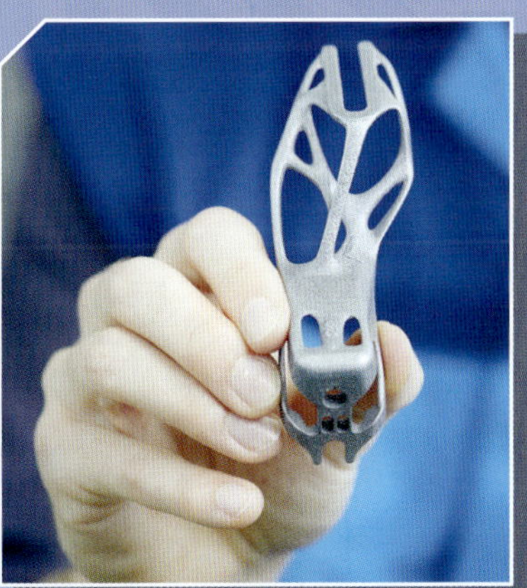

PRINTED PARTS
Modern car makers use 3D printing to create small, complex components with great precision. The process builds parts layer by layer from plastic or metal, guided by computer-controlled machines. This technology helps produce lightweight, strong pieces that would be hard to make using traditional methods.

DBS SUPERLEGGERA

The large honeycomb grille dominates the front of the car. It allows plenty of air into the engine.

Aston Martin's DBS Superleggera was the brand's flagship grand tourer - a larger, sharper, and more powerful version of the DB11. It stood as Aston's fastest and sleekest model from 2018 to 2024.

GRAND TOURER

A grand tourer (GT) is a large two-seater that combines high performance with a smooth driving experience. The engine of a GT is usually at the front to leave extra room for the cabin and a boot at the back. Aston Martin became famous in the 1950s for their luxurious, stylish and expensive GTs.

To give the car good grip, Aston Martin developed a system called the Aeroblade. Openings behind the rear windows trap air flowing on the side of the car. Ducts direct the air to the rear, where it leaves through a thin slit. The exiting air rushes out upwards, creating a force that presses down on the rear wheels.

DRIVING MODES

The DBS Superleggera can be driven in three different modes. The normal mode provides maximum comfort, with soft suspension for a smooth ride. The two sport modes stiffen up the suspension and make the steering more responsive. This gives a much bumpier ride, but improves the car's handling.

DBS SUPERLEGGERA

YEARS OF PRODUCTION:
2018–2024

ENGINE:
5.2 litre, 12 cylinders

POWER:
715 hp

TOP SPEED:
340 km/h

0–100 KM/H:
3.4 seconds

The luxurious seats are upholstered in soft leather.

SUPERCARS

Supercars are the ultimate dream rides with jaw-dropping power and futuristic designs. They are also very fast and expensive!

TOP SPEED RECORD FOR SUPERCARS SINCE 1967

YEAR	MODEL	TOP SPEED	POWER
1967	Lamborghini Miura P400	275 km/h	350 hp
1968	Ferrari 365 GTB/4 Daytona	280 km/h	352 hp
1969	Lamborghini Miura P400S	285 km/h	370 hp
1982	Lamborghini Countach LP500 S	293 km/h	375 hp
1983	Ruf BTR	300 km/h	369 hp
1986	Porsche 959	319 km/h	444 hp
1987	Ruf CTR	372 km/h	463 hp
1993	McLaren F1	355 km/h	627 hp
2004	Koenigsegg CCR	388 km/h	806 hp
2005	Bugatti Veyron EB	407.164 km/h	1,001 hp
2007	SSC Ultimate Aero	412.28 km/h	1,183 hp
2010	Bugatti Veyron 16.4 Super Sport	415 km/h	1,183 hp
2017	Koenigsegg Agera RS	447.19 km/h	1,341 hp

WHAT IS A SUPERCAR?

A supercar is a sports car that is very powerful and very fast. Supercars are production cars, but they are made in very small numbers. They are built using the cutting-edge technology found in racing cars, and are very expensive, often costing more than £1 million.

FAMOUS COLLECTORS

Supercars are often bought by collectors who have many different cars. Prince Rainer III of Monaco (1923–2005) assembled a huge collection of cars during his lifetime, including several supercars. They are now on display in a museum in Monaco.

A 1995 Ferrari F50 GT at the Monaco Top Cars Collection Museum, which displays the car collection of Prince Rainier III.

You're unlikely to spot a rare car like the Lamborghini Reventón (above) on the road, but supercar fans can check out all the very latest models at the Goodwood Festival of Speed, held each summer at Goodwood House in Britain. During the Supercar Run, manufacturers show off the power of their cars by testing them out with a timed hill climb.

REAR ENGINE
As in most supercars, the One:1's engine is at the rear. Side vents allow air in to cool it.

HYPERCARS

Some supercars are so exceptional in both performance and price that a new term has been invented for them. These are the even more exclusive hypercars. The Koenigsegg One:1 is a hypercar. Just six of them were made!

LAMBORGHINI MIURA

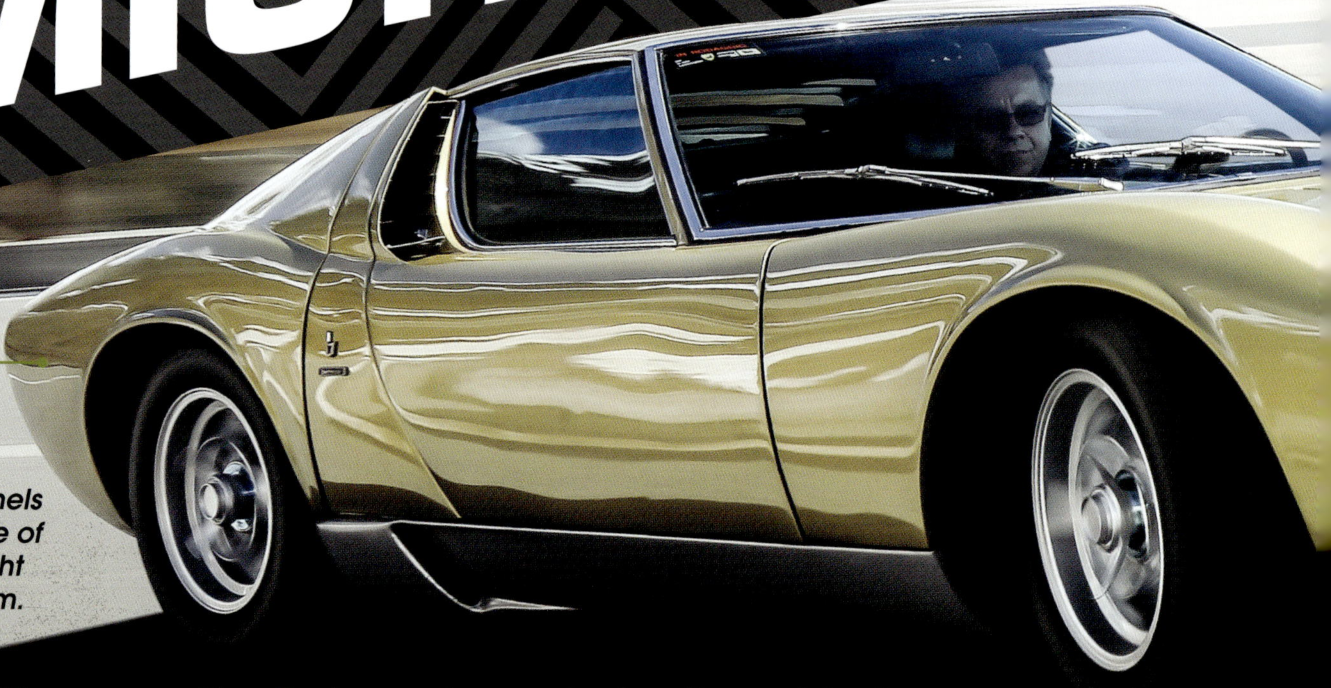

Body panels are made of lightweight aluminium.

The Miura was the first sports car to be thought of as a supercar. With its central V12 engine and streamlined design, it brought a racing car's performance to the road.

MIURA

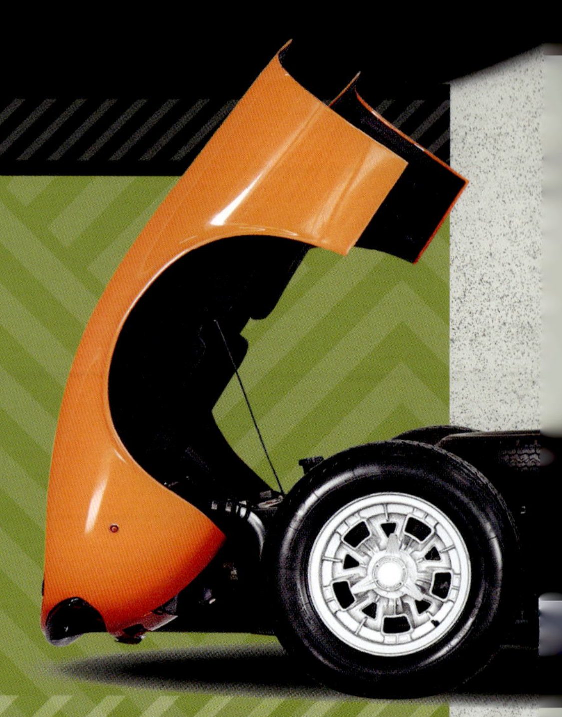

YEARS OF PRODUCTION:
1966–1973

NUMBER BUILT:
764

PRICE IN 1966:
£10,000
(£120,000 equivalent in 2020)

ENGINE:
3.9 litre, 12 cylinders

POWER:
350 hp

TOP SPEED:
280 km/h

0–100 KM/H:
6.7 seconds

SECRET PROJECT

The Miura was developed in 1965 by three of Lamborghini's senior engineers in their spare time. They had trouble convincing their boss, Ferruccio Lamborghini, that there was a market for such an expensive car. By the time the **prototype** was shown at the 1966 Geneva Motor Show, Lamborghini had been won over. It entered production soon after.

The headlights have distinctive 'eyelashes'.

GIAN PAOLO DALLARA

Lamborghini's first chief car designer, Gian Paolo Dallara (born 1936), worked on the **chassis** design of the Miura, and helped to establish the company as a leader in high-performance road cars. Later, he turned to racing cars, setting up his own company, Dallara Automobili, in 1972.

CHANGING GEAR

The Miura was fitted with a five-speed manual **gearbox**, operated by a leather gearstick.

MID-ENGINED CAR

The Miura was the first high-performance sports car to have a mid-engined, two-seater layout. Moving the engine from the front of the car places more weight on the rear wheels. This helps the car to grip the road when accelerating or taking corners. It is now the standard design for nearly all supercars.

BMW
M1

Developed in collaboration with Lamborghini, the M1 was BMW's first mid-engine car. It was produced for racing, but 460 road-going models were made in order to meet the requirements to enter the car for touring car race categories.

The body was made from lightweight fibreglass.

RACING SERIES

In 1979 and 1980, BMW ran a racing series in which all drivers used an identical M1 car. The series was a pure test of driving ability and it attracted many of the top Formula 1 stars. The first championship was won by Austrian Niki Lauda and the second by Brazilian Nelson Piquet, both of whom were also multiple F1 champions.

This is the M1 driven by Nelson Piquet in 1980. For racing, the M1 was fitted with a low front spoiler, wide wheel arches and an adjustable rear wing.

M1

*The wheels were made from a specially developed **alloy**.*

The M1 was built around a space-frame chassis. Designed by Lamborghini, the spaceframe was a strong but light structure made of steel tubing. Many high-performance racing cars are made with a spaceframe, but they are difficult to engineer and require extensive testing.

YEARS OF PRODUCTION:
1978–1981

NUMBER BUILT:
460

PRICE IN 1978:
£40,000 (£200,000 equivalent in 2020)

ENGINE:
3.5 litre, 6 cylinders

POWER:
277 hp

TOP SPEED:
265 km/h

0–100 KM/H:
5.6 seconds

*The bodywork, interior, engine, **transmission** and **suspension** were all attached to the tubular spaceframe.*

MCLAREN

F1

In 1992, champion Formula 1 team McLaren built their first production car. Using the latest racing technology and knowhow, they created the F1, the fastest road-legal car of its time.

RACING LOOK

The car's layout looks very similar to that of a racing car. The driver sits in the middle, creating a central driving position that maximises the car's stability at high speeds. While it is road-legal, the F1 is built for speed, and at the 1995 24 Hours of Le Mans race, a modified F1 beat purpose-built racing cars to claim the overall title.

The 'butterfly' doors open vertically around a front hinge.

AFTERCARE

Each of the 106 cars was custom built for its owner. While production stopped in 1998, owners can still call upon McLaren engineers who have been specially trained to maintain this model. If necessary, an engineer will fly out to a remote location to fix the car.

F1

YEARS OF PRODUCTION:
1992–1998

NUMBER BUILT:
106

PRICE IN 1992:
£600,000
($1.2 million equivalent in 2020)

ENGINE:
6.1 litre, 12 cylinders

POWER:
618 hp

0–100 KM/H:
3.2 seconds

TOP SPEED:
386.4 km/h

The car holds three people. The driver sits in the middle, with one passenger on either side.

Moulded monocoque is light but very strong.

TECH POINT

McLaren used Formula 1 technology to create a light but incredibly strong **monocoque** chassis/body for the F1. The chassis and body are created from one piece of moulded carbon-composite rather than body panels attached to a frame. This saves weight and also allows the car to be moulded into an **aerodynamic** and stylish shape. In this way, McLaren engineers were able to hit the target weight of just 1,018 kg, maximising the car's top speed.

BUGATTI
VEYRON

Designed and engineered by German company Volkswagen and built by French manufacturer Bugatti, the Veyron took over the mantle of fastest production car from the McLaren F1 in 2005. With a huge engine and sturdy body, the Veyron is large, loud and extremely powerful.

HUGE ENGINE

Bugattis are the only production cars in the world to feature a W16 engine, in which 16 cylinders are arranged in a 'W' shape. Turbochargers force compressed air into the engine to keep it running efficiently. At top speed, the engine needs 45,000 litres of air per minute to burn enough fuel. That's as much air as a human breathes in four days. At full throttle, it burns a litre of fuel every 10 seconds.

Four turbochargers force air into the 16 cylinders.

Slovak designer Jozef Kabaň (born 1973) was a rising young star at Volkswagen when he designed the exterior of the Bugatti Veyron. He later worked for Audi, Skoda and BMW, and is now at MG Motor as Vice President of the Global Design Centre.

The aluminium front grille allows air into the radiator.

VEYRON

YEARS OF PRODUCTION:
2005–2015

NUMBER BUILT:
450

PRICE:
£1.5 million

ENGINE:
8 litre, 16 cylinders

POWER:
1,001 hp (standard version)

0–100 KM/H:
2.46 seconds

TOP SPEED:
408 km/h

SUPER SPORT

In 2010, Bugatti brought out a limited edition of the Veyron called the Super Sport. By adding larger turbochargers, Bugatti's engineers managed to increase the power to 1,200 hp, and the Super Sport was recorded on the track at a record-breaking top speed of 431 km/h. On the road, it is limited to 415 km/h to protect the tyres from wear.

Unlike most supercars, the engine is placed just in front of the driver.

Lexus, the luxury car division of Japanese manufacturer Toyota, released its first supercar in 2010. The LFA may not be the fastest supercar ever made, but thanks to its smooth engine, it is one of the most pleasurable to drive.

Bumpers are made from reinforced panels.

NÜRBURGRING PACKAGE

Fifty of the 500 LFAs were made in a special racing 'Nürburgring package'. With 10 mm lower suspension, an added rear wing and side spoilers, they were designed to provide extra **downforce** at high speed. This makes for a less comfortable ride, but is perfect for owners to test their car on the track.

HIGH-TECH BODY

To make the body of the LFA, Lexus borrowed the latest aerospace technology. Two-thirds of the body was made from carbon fibre reinforced plastic (CFRP), and a third from aluminium. The carbon fibres were woven together in specially made high-tech looms.

The CFRP used in the body is lighter than aluminium, but four times stronger.

Side air intakes cool the brakes and the rear radiator.

LFA

YEARS OF PRODUCTION:
2010–2012

NUMBER BUILT:
500

PRICE:
£300,000

ENGINE:
4.8 litre, 10 cylinders

POWER:
553 hp

TOP SPEED:
325 km/h

0–100 KM/H:
3.7 seconds

TECH POINT

Lexus developed the roaring V10 engine especially for the LFA. With slightly smaller cylinders than a V8 engine of the same size, it can operate at upto 9,000 **revolutions per minute (rpm)**. This high rpm gives the engine a fast response time. It can move from zero to maximum rpm in just over half a second.

HUAYRA

YEARS OF PRODUCTION:
2011–2018

NUMBER BUILT:
100

PRICE:
£1 million

Italian manufacturer Pagani teamed up with engine-supplier Mercedes-AMG to produce a god of the wind, and its sleek, aerodynamic shape was inspired by the wing of an aircraft.

The Huayra is fitted with four aerodynamic flaps: two at the front and two at the back. They can all move independently, like the flaps on an aircraft wing. When the car brakes, all four flaps pop up to increase **drag**. When taking corners, only the flaps on the inside of the curve are raised. This increases the grip on the inside wheels, where it is most needed.

Leaf-shaped wing mirrors on carbon-fibre 'stalks'

DEVELOPING THE DESIGN

The Huayra spent around eight years in development, as Pagani engineers strove to create a car that would give the driver the feeling of brute force generated by an airplane at take-off. To produce the acceleration needed, the car had to be both powerful and as light as possible. Pagani tested eight scale models and two full-size models before finalising the design.

SPECIAL EDITIONS

Several customers have ordered specially made one-off versions of the Huayra. These include the Carbon Edition (below), which has a body and wheels made entirely from carbon fibre, and the Huayra Pearl, which has a more powerful engine and lighter weight.

TOP SPEED:
383 km/h

ENGINE:
6 litre, 12 cylinders

POWER:
730 hp

0 – 100 KM/H:
2.8 seconds

FERRARI
LAFERRARI

The LaFerrari was Ferrari's first hybrid hypercar – a major technological leap for the brand, blending Formula 1 hybrid tech with a road car. Only 499 were made, making it highly collectable.

LAFERRARI

Large side air intakes

YEARS OF PRODUCTION:
2013–2016

NUMBER MADE:
499

PRICE:
£1.2 million

ENGINE:
6.3 litre, 12 cylinders

POWER:
950 hp

TOP SPEED:
Over 350 km/h

0–100 KM/H:
2.6 seconds

HIGH-TECH BRAKES
The LaFerrari is fitted with brake discs made from a mix of carbon fibres and ceramic. The mixture was developed by Italian brake specialists Brembo. The discs create less heat than conventional metal brake discs and also save weight.

HYBRID ENGINE

The car is powered primarily by the engine, but the electric motor can give short bursts of extra power when it accelerates. The motor's battery contains 120 high-voltage cells, which are charged by recovering energy when the car brakes. The cells are also charged by the engine whenever it is producing more turning force, or **torque**, than is needed to turn the wheels, such as when it is taking corners.

The engine is kept cool by a system of water pipes.

Wide, low bonnet

RACING KNOWHOW

The engineers who designed the LaFerrari drew on the experience of legendary F1 racing car designer Rory Byrne (born 1944) to produce a structure that combined minimum weight, which is good for speed, with maximum rigidity, which is good for handling. In his years as Ferrari's chief designer, Byrne designed 11 different cars. His F1-designed cars have won 99 Grand Prix, seven Constructors' titles and seven Drivers' titles.

LYKAN HYPERSPORT

Designed by Lebanese engineers and built in Dubai by W Motors, the Lykan Hypersport is the first sports car to be designed and made in the Middle East. With just seven cars made in total, it is one of the most exclusive supercars ever produced.

PRECIOUS JEWELS

The Lykan Hypersport is the ultimate vehicle of luxurious excess. The headlights are encrusted with 420 diamonds, and customers could add rubies, sapphires and emeralds to change their colour.

In the centre of the car, next to the driver, is a 3D holographic display console. It is interactive, allowing the driver to operate the **GPS** navigation system or change the music with just a wave of the hand.

HYPERSPORT

YEARS OF PRODUCTION:
2013–2016

NUMBER BUILT:
7

PRICE:
£2.7 million

ENGINE:
3.7 litre, 6 cylinders

POWER:
781 hp

TOP SPEED:
395 km/h

0–100 KM/H:
2.9 seconds

POLICE CAR
The Abu Dhabi police force bought a Lykan Hypersport in 2015. It became fully operational four years later, fitted with flashing lights that somewhat spoil the car's aerodynamic design.

PORSCHE
918 SPYDER

The 918 Spyder is a high-performance hybrid sports car, powered by a petrol engine and two electric motors. It can run on just the engine when out on the open road, or it can glide silently and emission-free using only the electric motors in the city.

The car is shaped to allow air to flow over, under and through it as aerodynamically as possible. It is fitted with an active aerodynamic system made up of the rear wing, flaps in the underbody and air intakes under the headlights. These are constantly adjusted to ensure best performance.

The underbody is fully enclosed so that air flows smoothly under the car.

RACING BALANCE

The design of the 918 Spyder was inspired by racing technology. Its monocoque chassis is made from weight-saving carbon fibre reinforced plastic, while the heavier components, including the engine and battery, are placed as centrally and deeply as possible. This creates a very low centre of gravity, with slightly more weight towards the rear of the car, which helps it to grip the road when cornering at high speeds.

Electric motors are fitted to the front and rear axles.

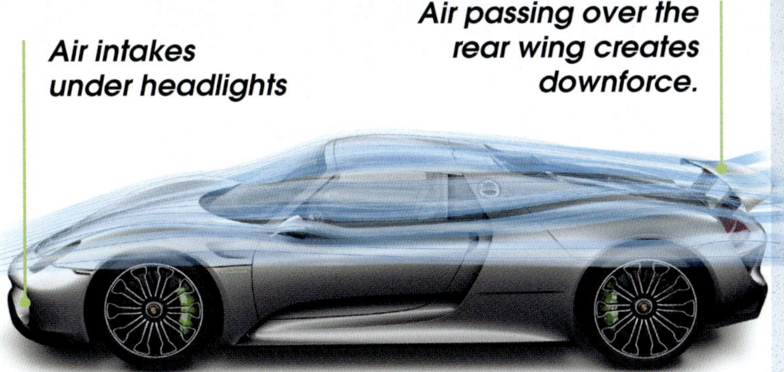

Air intakes under headlights

Air passing over the rear wing creates downforce.

918 SPYDER

YEARS OF PRODUCTION:
2013–2015

NUMBER BUILT:
918

PRICE:
£670,000

ENGINE:
4.6 litre, 8 cylinders, plus two electric motors

POWER:
887 hp

TOP SPEED:
345 km/h

0–100 KM/H:
2.6 seconds

TRACK RECORD

In 2013, Porsche demonstrated the speed and agility of the 918 Spyder by testing out a racing version on the Nürburgring track in Germany. It completed one lap of the 20.6-kilometre circuit in 6 minutes, 57 seconds, becoming the first road-legal car to break the 7-minute barrier.

RIMAC
CONCEPT ONE

The Concept One, made in Croatia by Rimac Automobili, is widely regarded as the world's first all-electric supercar. With around 1,088 hp – comparable to a Bugatti Veyron – it was the fastest accelerating electric vehicle when introduced.

CONTROLLED POWER

With a separate motor turning each wheel, the car can switch from front-wheel drive to rear-wheel drive or four-wheel drive, depending on the driving conditions. Rimac designed and built the electrical systems needed for the precise control of high-performance cars from scratch, taking out 24 patents on new technologies along the way.

Croatian engineer Mate Rimac started converting petrol cars into electric ones as a hobby. He won races driving his converted electric cars, and this attracted the attention of investors. With the money in place, he founded Rimac Automobili in 2009 to pursue his ambition to create the first electric high-performance car.

ONGOING DEVELOPMENT

The first Concept One was completed in January 2013, with 8 units produced by November 2014. Rimac unveiled a refined production version – including numerous upgrades – in March 2016 at the Geneva Motor Show. In July 2017, a Concept One set a new fastest electric car time at the Goodwood Hill Climb. By 2017, its official range was rated at about 330 km on a single charge. Rimac has since indicated plans for future models to exceed 500 km of electric range.

CONCEPT ONE

YEARS OF PRODUCTION:
2013–2014

NUMBER BUILT:
8

PRICE:
£800,000

MOTORS:
4 electric motors, powered by a 90 kWh battery

POWER:
1,224 hp

TOP SPEED:
355 km/h

0–100 KM/H:
2.6 seconds

KOENIGSEGG

AGERA RS

The Agera RS was declared the fastest production car ever when it was tested in 2017. Although it is completely road-legal, it contains many features designed for optimum performance on the track.

The low front spoiler creates downforce.

AGERA RS

YEARS OF PRODUCTION:
2015–2018

NUMBER BUILT:
25

POWER:
1,160 hp

PRICE:
£2 million

TOP SPEED:
458 km/h

ENGINE:
5 litre, 8 cylinders

0–100 KM/H:
2.9 seconds

The wing is operated by lightweight carbon rods.

ACTIVE WING

The rear wing changes angle automatically as the car moves. When the brakes are applied, it points up at 25 degrees, an angle that produces both drag to slow the car down and downforce to keep it on the road. At high speeds, it lies almost flat to minimise drag.

The body is made of lightweight carbon fibre.

CHRISTIAN VON KOENIGSEGG

Koenigsegg was founded in Sweden in 1994 by 22-year-old engineer Christian von Koenigsegg. Eight years later, the company produced its first street-legal production car, the CC8S. It has since won a reputation for innovation – developing and building its own components. The company has a large engineering department, led by von Koenigsegg.

HOLLOW WHEELS

Koenigsegg were the first manufacturer to fit production cars with carbon-fibre wheels. The Agera's 'Aircore' wheels are each made from one piece of light carbon fibre. They are hollow, saving about 20 kg in weight.

VENOM F5

US company Hennessey took the Venom F5 into production in 2020 with the aim of making the fastest road-legal car ever. The F5 is named after the highest rating on the Fujita scale for tornadoes.

The chassis and body are made of carbon fibre.

NEED FOR SPEED

Founder John Hennessey started his company to modify supercars and make them even faster. The first Hennessey supercar, the Venom GT, was a modified Lotus Exige and it set unofficial speed records. The F5 is the first car Hennessey will have built from scratch, and the goal is to take the official record this time.

VENOM F5

YEARS OF PRODUCTION:
2020–

NUMBER BUILT:
24

PRICE:
£1.6 million

ENGINE:
6.6 litre, 8 cylinders

The key to the Venom F5's speed is its 6.6-litre twin-turbocharged V8 engine, producing 1,817 hp in customer cars. Hennessey has tested the engine at over 2,000 hp and it held together!

Two huge turbochargers boost the engine's power.

FASTER THAN F1

The company aims to build the fastest-accelerating road car ever, targeting 300 km/h from a standing start in under 10 seconds – faster than a Formula 1 car – though this remains an ambitious goal.

The rear wing lowers when the car accelerates to improve its aerodynamics.

POWER:
Restricted to 1,817 hp

TOP SPEED:
484 km/h (ultimate goal)

0–100 KM/H:
2.6 seconds

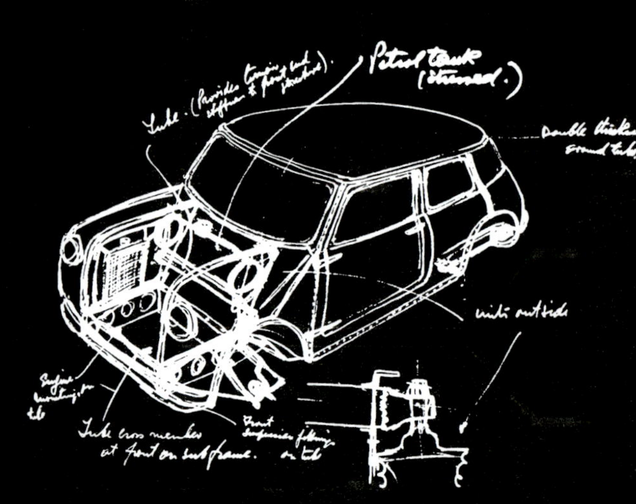

CLASSIC CARS

Welcome to the classics – timeless beauties that tell stories from the past.

RARE CLASSIC CARS SOMETIMES COME UP AT PUBLIC AUCTIONS. HERE ARE SOME OF THE BIGGEST PRICES THEY HAVE FETCHED.

CAR	YEAR FIRST MADE	YEAR SOLD	SALE PRICE
Rolls-Royce Silver Ghost	1907	2016	US$990,000
Lincoln KB Dual-Cowl Sport Phaeton	1932	2018	US$128,800
Volkswagen Beetle	1945	2016	US$121,000
Citroën DS23 convertible	1973	2009	US$440,000
Plymouth Fury	1956	2015	US$198,000
BMC Mini beach car	1962	2014	US$181,500
Jaguar E-Type	1961	2017	US$7.37 million
Porsche 911 Carrera 2.7 RS	1972	2015	US$1.4 million
Ford Mustang Shelby GT500 Super Snake	1967	2019	US$2.2 million
Toyota 2000GT	1967	2013	US$1.2 million
Ferrari Dino 246 GTS	1973	2019	US$555,000
BMW E9 3.0 CSL	1971	2018	US$400,000

WHAT IS A CLASSIC CAR?

Classic cars are old models that people enjoy owning, restoring and collecting. Some are very rare and change hands for huge sums of money. Owners of classic cars take great care of their vehicles to keep them in their original condition.

Many classic car owners bring their vehicles out each year at the Rally of Vintage Cars in Barcelona, which is exclusively for cars made before 1924.

CLASSIC OR VINTAGE?

Any car model that is not made any more may be called a classic if enough people still want to own it. However, most classic cars are at least 40 years old. Cars made before the 1940s are also called vintage cars. These very old cars need a lot of maintenance to keep them in working order.

Vintage Volkswagen Beetles at a rally in New York.

MOVIE STARS

Some cars achieve classic status with the help of movie appearances. British sports car manufacturer Aston Martin have provided a car for 12 different James Bond movies. Their first appearance came in the 1964 film *Goldfinger*. Aston Martin made two models of the DB5 for the film, one of which was fitted with gadgets for Bond to use.

CLASSIC RESTORATION

Old cars in poor condition can be bought cheaply and restored. For many owners, working on an old wreck is a labour of love. The engines may need to be rebuilt, replacing worn-out components. Restoring the bodywork can take hundreds of hours of work. Dents must be hammered out, while some panels may need replacing. The whole thing needs to be repainted at the end.

ROLLS-ROYCE
SILVER GHOST

First made in 1907, the Silver Ghost is the car that established British company Rolls-Royce as the leading luxury car manufacturer. It was described at the time as 'the best car in the world'.

SPIRIT OF ECSTASY

At the front of the bonnet of Rolls-Royce cars sits the Spirit of Ecstasy emblem. It takes the form of a woman leaning forwards with her arms outstretched as if she had wings. Designed by sculptor Charles Sykes, it has featured on every Rolls-Royce car since 1911.

TECH POINT

In 1907, Rolls Royce demonstrated the reliability of their new model by driving it between London and Glasgow 27 times – a distance of 24,000 km. Engineers checked the car at the end of the test and found that the engine was still in good working order.

*The engine contained six large **cylinders** in one line.*

QUIET RUNNING

Rolls-Royce originally called the car the 40/50 hp, after its power capabilities. However, this name proved to be too dull, and journalists soon nicknamed it the 'Silver Ghost' after the colour of the first model and the smooth, quiet running of its engine.

YEARS OF PRODUCTION:
1907–1926

NUMBER BUILT:
7,874 (around 1,500 still survive)

ENGINE:
7 litre, 6 cylinders

POWER:
48 hp

TOP SPEED:
125 km/h

TODAY'S VALUE:
Up to £30 million

The folding roof was made of black canvas.

PRIZED POSSESSION
Surviving models of the Silver Ghost are some of the most valuable cars in the world. The car that was tested in 1907 is still in working order more than a century later, and is thought to be worth more than £30 million.

LINCOLN
K SERIES

The K Series was a line of luxury cars produced by American manufacturer Lincoln. These elegant cars were popular among Hollywood stars in the 1930s.

Low, sloping windscreen

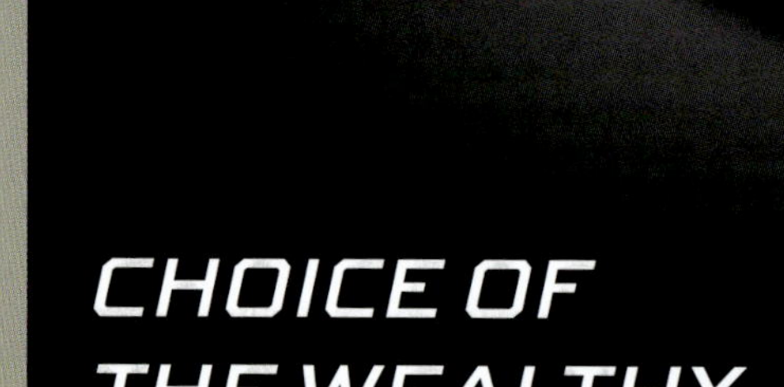

K SERIES

YEARS OF PRODUCTION:

1931–1940

ENGINE:

6.3 litre, 12 cylinders or
7.3 litre, 12 cylinders

POWER:

150 hp (V12 model)

TOP SPEED:

161 km/h (V12 model)

TODAY'S VALUE:

£40,000–£80,000
depending on the model

CHOICE OF THE WEALTHY

The K Series came in many different styles and options, allowing Lincoln's wealthy clients to customise their vehicles. Many were designed to be driven by a **chauffeur**, with a driver's compartment that was separated from the rest of the car.

Cars in the 1930s had narrow bodies that sat high off the ground. They were fitted with running boards to help people to climb in and out. Lincoln made their running boards into a stylish feature, sweeping back from the front mudguards. The boards could also be used to carry luggage or even pets!

A detachable rack could be fitted above the small boot to provide extra space for luggage.

SUNSHINE SPECIAL

In 1939, Lincoln built a special edition of the K Series for US President Franklin D Roosevelt to use as his official state car. It was nicknamed the 'Sunshine Special' after its retractable roof, which Roosevelt liked to keep open during public appearances.

VOLKSWAGEN BEETLE

With more than 21 million built in nearly 70 years of production, the Volkswagen Beetle was the most popular car ever made. Its overall shape remained almost unchanged over the decades, but the engine and other mechanical systems were updated as technology improved.

FERDINAND PORSCHE

The Beetle was designed by Austrian engineer Ferdinand Porsche (1875–1951), founder of the Porsche sports car manufacturer. Porsche placed the engine at the rear and created an **aerodynamic** shape for the Beetle. Today, Porsche is a divisive figure in Germany due to his close association with the Nazis.

THE PEOPLE'S CAR

The word Volkswagen means 'people's car'. The Beetle was commissioned by the Nazi German Chancellor Adolf Hitler, who wanted a cheap, reliable car that could carry a family of four and maintain a speed of 100 km/h on Germany's new motorways. It was first made in 1938, but mass production did not start until 1946, after the Second World War (1939–45).

Bumpers wear out and need to be replaced every few years. They can still be bought from specialist suppliers.

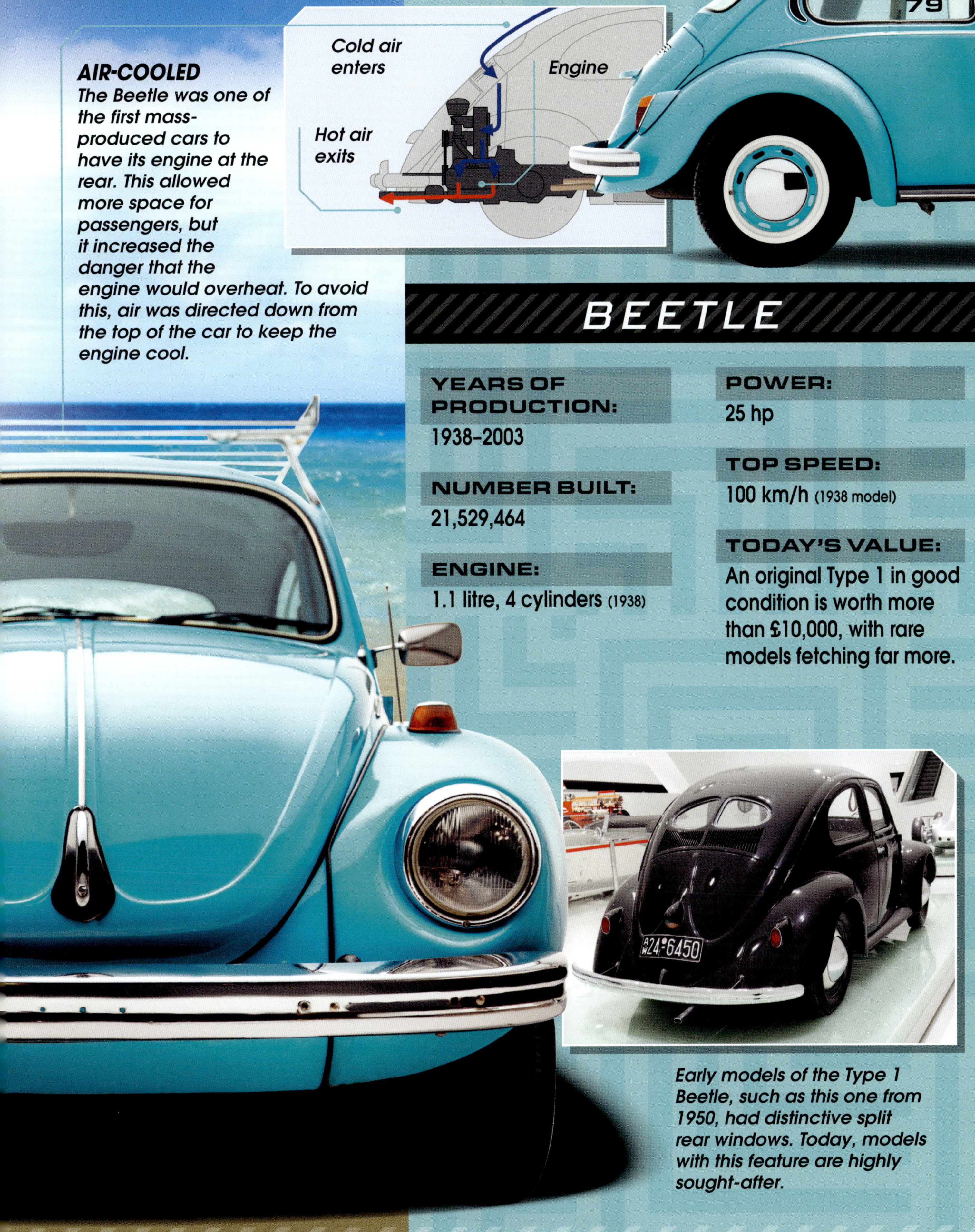

AIR-COOLED

The Beetle was one of the first mass-produced cars to have its engine at the rear. This allowed more space for passengers, but it increased the danger that the engine would overheat. To avoid this, air was directed down from the top of the car to keep the engine cool.

BEETLE

YEARS OF PRODUCTION:
1938–2003

NUMBER BUILT:
21,529,464

ENGINE:
1.1 litre, 4 cylinders (1938)

POWER:
25 hp

TOP SPEED:
100 km/h (1938 model)

TODAY'S VALUE:
An original Type 1 in good condition is worth more than £10,000, with rare models fetching far more.

Early models of the Type 1 Beetle, such as this one from 1950, had distinctive split rear windows. Today, models with this feature are highly sought-after.

DS

First made in 1955, the Citroën DS was an executive car packed with the latest technology. In French, its name sounds like the word 'déesse', meaning goddess, and it soon became a symbol of French innovation and style.

ANDRÉ LEFÈBVRE

Three of Citroën's most successful cars were created by André Lefèbvre (1894–1964). In addition to the DS, he designed the Traction Avant, the first front-wheel-drive production car, and the 2CV, a small car introduced in 1948 to compete with the VW Beetle. Before joining Citroën, Lefèbvre had a successful career as a racing car driver.

HIGH-TECH SUSPENSION
To deal with France's bumpy roads, the DS was fitted with a self-levelling *suspension* operated by *hydraulics*. The suspension could adjust itself on each wheel independently to keep the car level.

On the 1967 DS, headlights rotated to point in the same direction as the front wheels.

NEW IDEAS

In addition to its innovative suspension system, the DS was the first production car to feature **disc brakes**. It was also fitted with a hydraulically controlled **gearbox**, meaning that there was no need for a **clutch** pedal. The wheels at the front were wider apart than those at the rear, which improved the handling.

DS

YEARS OF PRODUCTION:
1955–1975

ENGINE:
1.9–2.3 litre, 4 cylinders

POWER:
75 hp (1955 model)
141 hp (1972 model)

TOP SPEED:
145 km/h

TODAY'S VALUE:
from £30,000

When the engine was switched on, the hydraulics raised the whole car up.

FURY

The Plymouth Fury has become a symbol of 1950s America. Big, heavy and with an engine that guzzled petrol, this executive car was made at a time when fuel was cheap and style was important.

Curved windows resemble those of a jet plane's cockpit.

FURY

YEARS OF PRODUCTION:
1955–1961 (original version)

ENGINE:
5–5.9 litre, 8 cylinders

POWER:
up to 305 hp

TOP SPEED:
220 km/h

TODAY'S VALUE:
up to £50,000

Huge chrome-plated front bumper and grille

SPACE-AGE STYLE

Like many American cars in the 1950s, the Fury was fitted with two large tailfins. They were shaped to resemble the engine sections of jet fighters or space rockets. Plymouth claimed that the tailfins helped to keep the car stable in cross winds, but, in reality, they were all about looks. Tailfins went out of fashion in the 1960s amid safety concerns about sharp parts on cars.

Chrome-plated trim pieces

Tailfin

CUBAN CLASSICS

Many classic 1950s American cars are still running on the roads in Cuba. Thousands of people immigrated to the USA following the Cuban Revolution of 1959, but they had to leave their American cars behind. Over time, the original parts have often been replaced with parts from other cars, such as engines from a Lada, a small car made in the Soviet Union.

STATION WAGON

An even bigger version of the Fury was available in the form of a station wagon. Also known as estates, these are cars with an extended rear to accommodate a larger boot. Today, they have largely been replaced by sport utility vehicles (SUVs).

BMC
MINI

The best-selling British car of all time, the Mini, was a small car famed for its space and handling. Designed to be basic and affordable, the Mini became a style icon in the 1960s and the original Mark 1 model is now a highly desirable collector's item.

FUEL CRISIS

In the late 1950s, Britain was experiencing an oil crisis and fuel was rationed. Sales of large cars collapsed, while small cars from Germany and Italy became very popular because they needed less fuel. The Mini was the British Motor Corporation's response to the crisis. It was economical, but still had space for four adults and gave a sharp, responsive drive, despite its small engine.

MINI

YEARS OF PRODUCTION:
1959–2000

ENGINE:
1.1 litre, 4 cylinders
(Mark 1)

SINGLE STRUCTURE

The Mini had a single **monocoque** body, a cutting-edge technology at the time that saved space.

The wheels were just 25 cm in diameter. This saved more space.

ALEC ISSIGONIS

Designer Alec Issigonis (1906–1988) created the shape of the Mini and was also responsible for developing its space-saving innovations. The guiding idea behind his designs was that people who drive small cars are the same size as those who drive large cars, and the cars need to reflect that.

Alec Issigonis' hand-drawn sketch shows his idea for a sideways-mounted engine.

Engine and gearbox

Passenger compartment

Boot space

POWER:
70 hp

TOP SPEED:
150 km/h

TODAY'S VALUE:
1960s cars sell for £10,000 or more

MAXIMUM SPACE

Eighty per cent of the Mini's area was used by passengers and luggage. To achieve this, the engine sat sideways at the front and the car was front-wheel drive. The suspension saved space by using rubber cones instead of springs. This made for a bumpy ride, but also gave excellent handling.

JAGUAR
E-TYPE

The E-Type is a two-seater sports car that combines high performance with style. The car was described by Enzo Ferrari, founder of the Ferrari motor racing team, as 'the most beautiful car ever made'.

Hard-top coupé

E-TYPE

YEARS OF PRODUCTION:
1961–1974

ENGINE:
3.8–4.2 litre, 6 cylinders (Series 1)

POWER:
265 hp

DASH TO GENEVA

The E-Type was first shown to the public at the 1961 Geneva Motor Show. Jaguar only took the coupé version, but it proved such a hit that they wanted to show off the open-top roadster (left). Test driver Norman Dewis jumped in the roadster version at the Jaguar factory in Coventry, England, and drove through the night to reach Geneva in 11 hours, covering a distance of 1,000 km.

Battery pack sits where the engine was.

MODERN TAKE

In 2018, Jaguar produced the E-Type Zero, replacing the E-Type's petrol engine with an electric motor. The motor and battery were the same size and weight as the original engine so that the car kept its perfect balance.

TECH POINT

The E-Type's distinctive long bonnet and sleek curves were created by Malcolm Sayer (1916–1970). An aircraft engineer during the Second World War, Sayer knew the importance of aerodynamics to high-speed performance. In the days before computer design, he used mathematical formulas to create the car's curves. He attached tufts of wool to the bonnet during testing to see how air flowed over it.

The display on the dashboard of the E-Type Zero shows how much battery power is left.

TOP SPEED:
240 km/h

0–100 KM/H:
7 seconds

TODAY'S VALUE:
from £100,000

PORSCHE

911

The 911 was designed by Butzi Porsche, grandson of the creator of the VW Beetle (see page 10). With more than 1 million cars made, the 911 has been in production since 1963, undergoing continuous improvements while its basic shape has remained the same.

911

Like the VW Beetle, the 911's engine is at the rear.

YEARS OF PRODUCTION:
1963–1989

ENGINE:
2–3.2 litre, 6 cylinder

POWER:
130 hp (1963)

TODAY'S VALUE:
From £20,000, up to £1 million for a Carrera RS 2.7

RACING SUCCESS

As well as being a road car, the original 911 series, produced from 1964 to 1989, was one of the most successful racing cars in history, winning titles both on the track and in off-road rallies. A heavily modified 911, known as the 935, won the Silverstone 6 Hours sports car **endurance race** in 1978.

*The 935 that won at Silverstone had a long tail and huge rear wing to produce maximum **downforce**. It was nicknamed 'Moby Dick'.*

The boot is at the front, under the bonnet.

TECH POINT

In 1966, Porsche improved the performance of the 911 by fitting its sports model with new lightweight wheels called Fuchs wheels. Made from a light aluminium **alloy**, the wheels were forged in one piece using a process invented by metal specialist Otto Fuchs. The weight saved gave the car a crucial advantage in track races.

PRIZED MODEL

While all original 911s are classic cars, some are much more valuable than others. One of the rarest and most sought after is the 1973 Carrera RS 2.7. This model was stripped of all inessential parts to produce a lightweight racing car that generated 210 hp.

FORD
MUSTANG

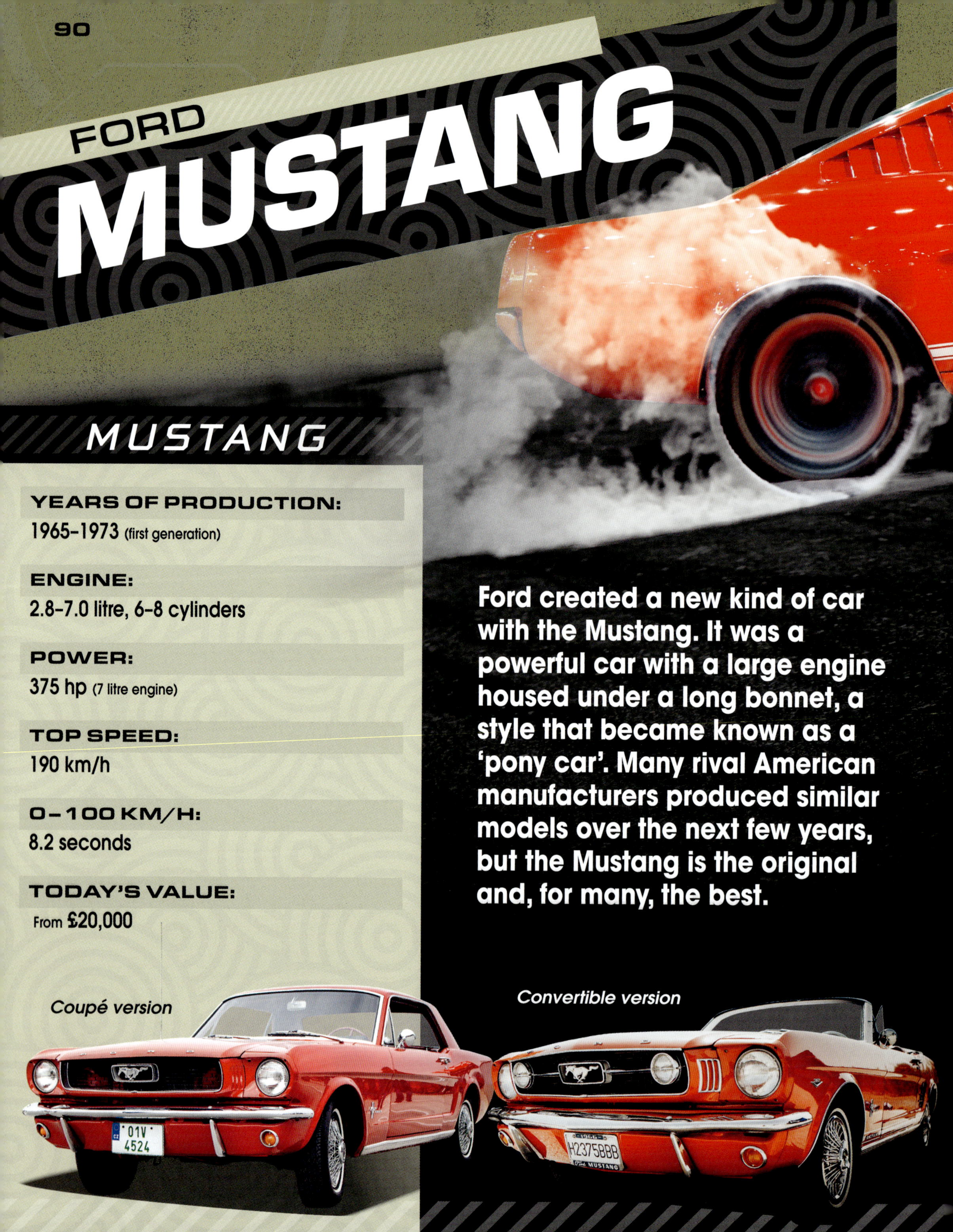

MUSTANG

YEARS OF PRODUCTION:
1965–1973 (first generation)

ENGINE:
2.8–7.0 litre, 6–8 cylinders

POWER:
375 hp (7 litre engine)

TOP SPEED:
190 km/h

0–100 KM/H:
8.2 seconds

TODAY'S VALUE:
From £20,000

Ford created a new kind of car with the Mustang. It was a powerful car with a large engine housed under a long bonnet, a style that became known as a 'pony car'. Many rival American manufacturers produced similar models over the next few years, but the Mustang is the original and, for many, the best.

Coupé version

Convertible version

The 'fastback' version of the Mustang had a sloping rear window and boot.

INSTANT HIT

The first generation of the Mustang was produced from 1965 to 1973. It proved an instant hit in the USA, with more than 1 million sold in the first 18 months of production. The car was revised several times, making it bigger and more powerful. It was replaced by the smaller, more economical Mustang II in 1974, following a rise in the price of petrol.

CLASSIC CHASE

The Mustang achieved worldwide fame in 1968 when it featured in the film Bullitt. Pursued by a Dodge Charger, it was involved in one of the longest car chases in film history. The chase lasted more than ten minutes on screen, and took three weeks to film.

TECH POINT

To develop their ideas for a pony car, Ford made two **concept cars**. The Mustang I, made in 1962, was a mid-engined car with a streamlined bonnet. Ford worried that it would be hard to make, so they created a front-engine version, the Mustang II, a year later. The Mustang II was a hit at car shows, and the car went into production shortly afterwards.

Mustang 1 concept car

TOYOTA
2000GT

This limited-edition sports car changed the world's perception of Japanese cars. Japan was known for vehicles that were more practical than stylish. The 2000GT was the exact opposite: beautiful but cramped.

The car was just 1.16 metres high.

Two narrow chrome bumpers protected the front and rear of the car.

RARE MODEL

Just 351 2000GTs were built, and it is widely thought of today as Japan's first **supercar**. Toyota treated it as a 'halo car', meaning that it lost them money but gave the company great publicity. Today, its rarity makes it extremely valuable, and one fully restored model sold in 2013 for £800,000.

BOND CAR

A one-off open-top roadster version of the 2000GT was built for the 1967 Bond movie You Only Live Twice. *The roof had to be removed because the actor playing James Bond, Sean Connery, was too tall to fit inside.*

The wheels were fitted with power-assisted disc brakes.

2000 GT

YEARS OF PRODUCTION:
1967–1970

ENGINE:
2.0–2.3 litre, 6 cylinders

POWER:
150 hp

TOP SPEED:
220 km/h

0–100 KM/H:
10 seconds

TODAY'S VALUE:
Up to £800,000

TECH POINT

Toyota designer Satoru Nozaki was influenced by the Jaguar E-Type (see pages 86–87) in his design for the 2000GT. He took the E-Type's basic shape and made it even more aerodynamic by shortening and narrowing it. He also lowered the nose and bonnet, which meant that the car had to be fitted with pop-up headlights to comply with the minimum height requirements in California, an important market for sports cars.

Pop-up headlights

DINO
246 GT

In 1969, Ferrari joined forces with fellow Italians Fiat to produce the Dino, a series of relatively affordable sports cars to rival Porsche's 911 (see pages 88-89). Today, the Dino 246 GT is worth far more than its original selling price.

The Dino 246 GT had softer, more rounded edges than a typical Ferrari.

NEW MARQUE
The Dino marque is named after the son of Enzo Ferrari, the company's founder. Alfredo 'Dino' Ferrari died in 1956, aged just 24. At the time, he had been working on a small V6 engine for Formula Two racing. His engine was used for the first Dino, the 206 GT.

Ferrari used the Dino engine from the late 1950s to the early 2000s. In the Ferrari Dino cars, the engine was placed sideways mid-car. This left little room for driver and passenger but gave the car excellent balance and allowed for a streamlined bonnet.

246 GT

YEARS OF PRODUCTION:
1969–1974

ENGINE:
2.4 litre, 6 cylinders

POWER:
195 hp

TOP SPEED:
235 km/h

TODAY'S VALUE:
£300,000

The interior was cramped, so there was no room for a glove compartment on the passenger side.

FIAT DINO
Fiat built the engine for the Ferrari Dino, and used it to make a Dino range of their own. They moved the engine to the front to allow more room inside. The Fiat Dino has also become a classic, and today it is worth up to £100,000.

BMW

E9

BMW's E9 was a range of high-performance two-door coupés. It was highly successful in touring car races, and helped to establish the German manufacturer's reputation for well-built, sporty executive cars.

Hofmeister kink

E9

YEARS OF PRODUCTION:
1968–1975

ENGINE:
2.5–3 litre, 6 cylinders

POWER:
205 hp (CSL)

DISTINCTIVE KINK

BMW cars have several distinctive design features that make them instantly recognisable. One of these is the 'Hofmeister kink', a curve in the back corner of the rear window. It was first introduced in 1961 by head of design Wilhelm Hofmeister, who was also in charge of the design of the E9. The kink has featured on nearly all BMW cars ever since.

The 3.0 CLS was fitted with a rear wing for racing.

TECH POINT

In 1972, BMW produced a special racing version of the E9 called the 3.0 CSL. The car was made as light as possible by stripping out the soundproofing, and using thinner steel for the body, aluminium for the doors, bonnet and boot, and Perspex for the side windows. Just 1,265 cars were built, and today the CSL is a rare collector's item.

TOP SPEED:
214 km/h (CSL)

TODAY'S VALUE:
£180,000 (CSL)

ART CAR
BMW have a tradition of asking famous artists to create one-off paint jobs for their cars. The first of these 'Art Cars' was an E9 3.0 CSL painted by American artist Alexander Calder. He chose the bright colours his artwork was known for. The car was raced at the 1975 24 Hours of Le Mans.

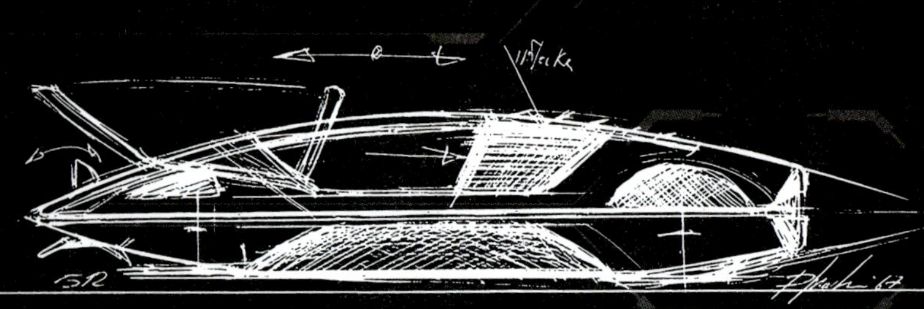

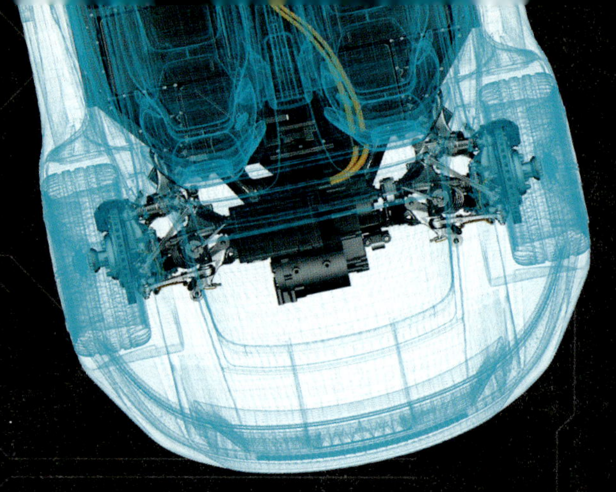

CONCEPT CARS

Finally, let's explore concept cars and ultimately what the future of cars might look like.

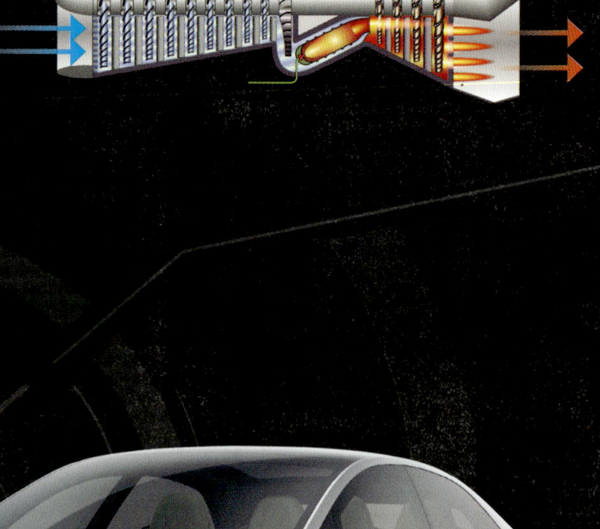

CONCEPT CARS AND THEIR LEGACIES

CAR	MANUFACTURER	YEAR MADE	LEGACY
Firebird 1	General Motors	1953	The aircraft-inspired turbine engine never took off.
Modulo	Ferrari	1970	Not made, but inspired many wedge-shaped sports cars.
Karin	Citroën	1980	Not made. Pyramid-shaped cars were not the future of design.
Prowler	Plymouth	1993	Went into production four years later.
Pivo	Nissan	2005	It was followed by the Pivo 2 and the Pivo 3 concepts. Small electric city cars are increasingly popular.
GINA	BMW	2008	Shape-shifting cars remain a futuristic dream.
Exalt	Peugeot	2014	High performance cars continue to be made using carbon fibre, not basalt fibre.
Mission E	Porsche	2015	Came into production as the Taycan in 2019. In a few years, all new cars are likely to be electric.
Trezor	Renault	2016	Not made, but aerodynamic electric sports cars are set to become increasingly common.
Terzo Millennio	Lamborghini	2017	Its idea for storing electrical energy may be a very good solution. Too early to say.
ID Vizzion	Volkswagen	2018	Fully autonomous cars are a reality, but we may not see them on the roads for a long time.

WHAT IS A CONCEPT CAR?

Concept cars are experimental vehicles that allow designers to let their imaginations run wild. Some of their ideas work, while others don't. Take a look at some of the strangest concept cars ever made.

At the 2018 Geneva Car Show, Renault showed off the EZ-GO, a futuristic design for a fully robotic self-driving car.

SHOWING OFF

Concept cars normally make their first appearance at a car show. This gives manufacturers the chance to explain their idea and see how well it is received. While the concept cars may not make it to production, many of the ideas that they showcase will be developed and appear in showrooms a few years later.

BUICK Y-JOB

The 1938 Buick Y-Job was the first concept car ever made. The brainchild of chief designer Harley Earl (pictured here behind the wheel), the Y-Job featured many new ideas, including hidden headlights, electric windows and wraparound bumpers.

While some concept cars are fully operational vehicles, others are so experimental that they are presented only as scale models or design sketches. Young American student Chris Chungkyo Lee (below) so impressed BMW with his futuristic iQ design that they gave him a job!

WACKY DESIGNS

Concept cars often challenge our ideas about what a car can be. In 2010, US manufacturer General Motors unveiled the EN-V, a pod-shaped two-seater vehicle for city driving. It featured a self-balancing system that allowed it to stay upright on just two wheels. This futuristic concept car featured in the Disney sci-fi film Tomorrowland (2015), but it has yet to appear on the road.

The EN-V is an electric car with just two wheels.

FIREBIRD

In the 1950s, General Motors produced three futuristic concept cars that were powered by jet engines. Appropriately named Firebird, they were like missiles on wheels, generating both incredible power and a dangerous amount of heat.

DANGEROUS JET

Firebird 1 was built in 1953. It had a tiny one-person cockpit, wings and a vertical tailfin. The car was powered by a gas turbine engine that blasted out exhaust fumes at nearly 700°C. In test runs, Firebird 1 was taken up to a speed of 160 km/h, at which point it started to take off, and the driver had to slam on the brakes!

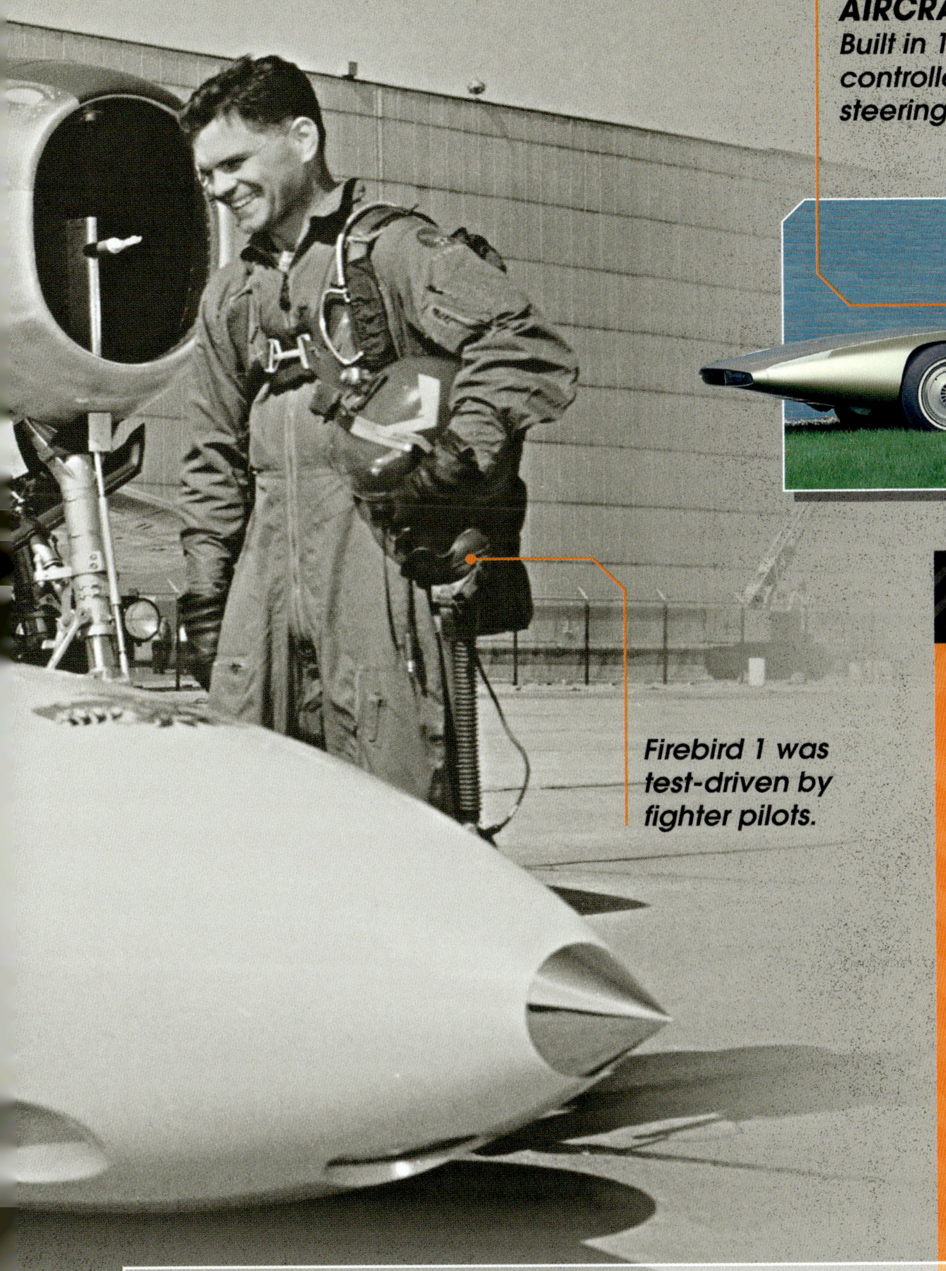

AIRCRAFT CONTROLS

Built in 1958, the two-seater Firebird 3 was controlled using a joystick rather than a steering wheel.

Firebird 1 was test-driven by fighter pilots.

FIREBIRD 1

YEAR CREATED:
1953

TOP SPEED:
320 km/h in theory, but too dangerous to take above 160 km/h

WEIGHT:
1,134 kg

POWER:
370 hp gas turbine engine

TECH POINT

Gas turbine engines produce power by forcing air through a **turbine**, or fan, causing it to spin at high speed. Today, gas turbine engines power aeroplanes, helicopters and tanks, but not cars!

1. Air is sucked in at the front and squeezed by a spinning compressor, increasing the pressure of the air.

2. The high-pressure air enters a combustion area where burning fuel heats it, creating even more pressure.

3. The hot air blasts at high speed through the turbine, causing it to spin. The energy from the turbine powers the vehicle.

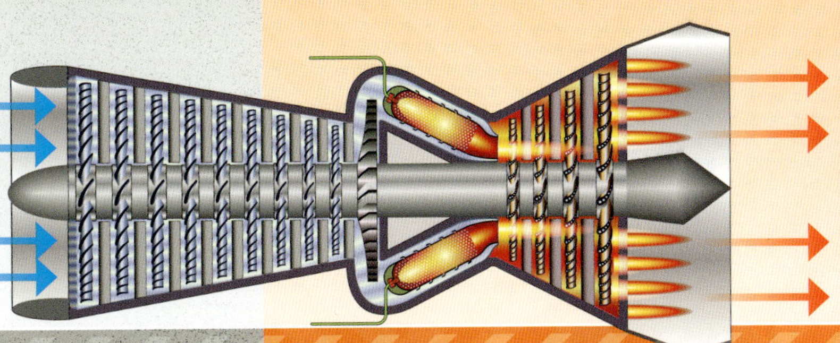

MODULO

Ferrari's Modulo was the ultimate 'wedge' design, made to cut through the air at high speed. This extreme sports car was only 93 cm high.

When it was displayed at the 1970 Geneva Motor Show, the Modulo did not have an engine, so it had to be pushed into place.

PAOLO MARTIN

The Modulo was the brainchild of 25-year-old designer Paolo Martin. Working by hand, Martin first sketched out his ideas for the car on a large sheet of paper. His extreme design was a big influence on other car designers and led to the production of many wedge-shaped sports cars in the 1970s.

Paolo Martin worked on these designs standing at a large drawing board.

CENTRAL ENGINE
The huge V12 engine (12 cylinders in a 'V' shape) sat near the centre to give the car balance and stability.

MODULO

YEAR CREATED:
1970

ENGINE:
5 litre V12

POWER:
550 hp

TOP SPEED:
350 km/h

0 – 100 KM/H:
3.2 seconds

WHERE IS IT NOW?
The Modulo spent decades without moving, on display in museums. The car finally hit the road in 2018 after it was bought by US motor enthusiast James Glickenhaus, who restored the car to full working order.

The wheels were all partially covered, which improved the car's aerodynamics.

LOW DOWN
The Modulo was so low that the entire roof, including the windscreen, had to slide forwards to allow the driver and passenger to climb in. Inside, they leaned back on specially moulded seats, which anchored the driver in the correct position to drive.

CITROËN
KARIN

The angular Karin from French manufacturer Citroën was a pyramid on wheels, with a flat roof no bigger than a sheet of A3 paper! This concept car was a styling exercise, made to show how cars might look in the future.

The pyramid shape gave the Karin a very low centre of gravity, making it very stable.

KARIN

YEAR CREATED:
1980

ENGINE:
4-cylinder (planned)

HEIGHT:
1.08 metres

WIDTH:
1.9 metres

Born Trevor Frost in England in 1937. Fiore moved to Turin, Italy, where he worked for car designer Carrozzeria Fissore, creating stylish sports cars such as the 1965 TVR Trident. By 1980, Fiore had become head of Citroën design. The Karin was his first project in the new job, designed for Citroën to display at the 1980 Paris Motor Show.

SHARP ANGLES

The cabin seated three people sat side-by-side. They were surrounded by glass, and the sharply angled panels allowed a full all-round view from inside. On a sunny day, the glass would act like a greenhouse, and the Karin was likely to get very hot. The pyramid design never did catch on.

The butterfly doors opened vertically.

CENTRAL DRIVER

The driver sat in the middle of the car, set back from the engine at the front. The long steering column allowed the driver to access nearly all of the controls without letting go of the steering wheel. Small computers were located by the door handles for the passengers to operate.

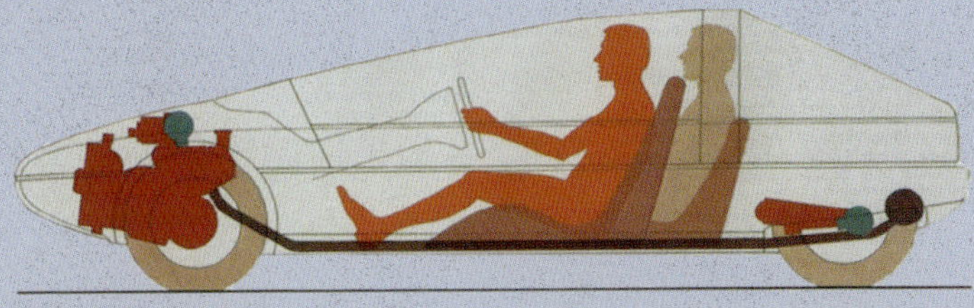

PLYMOUTH
PROWLER

In 1993, designers at US manufacturer Chrysler were asked to create a modern sports car that looked like the classic 'hot rods' of the 1930s. They came up with the Plymouth Prowler, a stylish design that proved such a hit at the 1993 Detroit Motor Show that it went into production four years later.

The Prowler was a roadster, which means that it was a two-seater with a removable roof. The roof folded down into the small boot, which didn't leave any room for luggage. When the model went on sale in 1997, it came with an option for a luggage trailer with matching wheels and tyres.

The V6 engine was relatively small, but the car's light weight gave it good acceleration.

The open front wheels were the most striking difference between the Prowler and most modern cars. The wheels were fitted with wide, curving mudguards, just like those found on the 1930s cars that inspired the design. Open wheels cause a lot of **drag**, so the mudguards also helped with the aerodynamics.

The narrow, pointed body and exposed wheels gave the car its retro feel.

STYLE OVER SPEED

With a retro design and relatively small engine, the Prowler couldn't keep up with modern sports cars in terms of speed or **acceleration**. However, its popularity led to the production of other retro designs in the early 2000s, such as the 2002 Ford Thunderbird.

PROWLER

YEAR CREATED:
1993 (entered production in 1997)

ENGINE:
3.5 litre V6

TOP SPEED:
190 km/h

WEIGHT:
1,270 kg

POWER
214 hp

0–100 KM/H:
7.2 seconds

NISSAN
PIVO

Ask drivers what their least favourite manoeuvre is, and most will answer: 'parking'. In 2005, Japanese manufacturer Nissan came up with a revolutionary solution!

PIVO

YEAR CREATED:
2005

WEIGHT:
1,000 kg

POWER:
Electric motor

TOP SPEED:
100 km/h

NO GOING BACK!
The egg-shaped cabin could rotate to any angle, meaning that the car had no need for a reverse gear. When parking in a tight space, the driver simply turned the cabin and wheels around to face the other way. The car was symmetrical in its design, so it looked exactly the same to the driver when the cabin was turned 180 degrees.

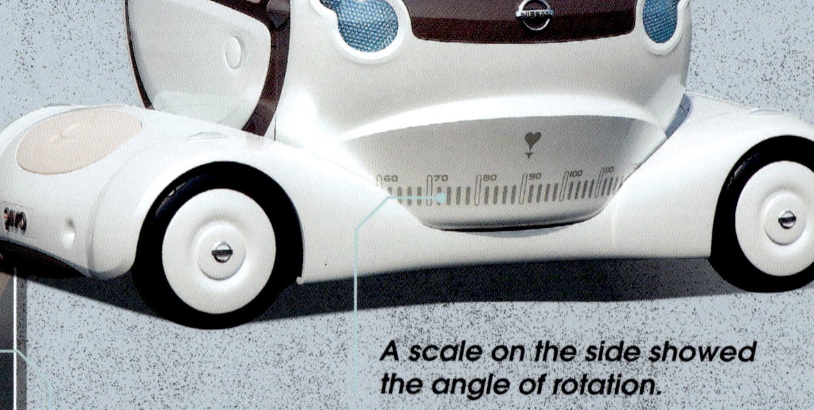

A scale on the side showed the angle of rotation.

CITY CAR
There was no back seat, and the driver sat in the centre in between the two passengers. Easy to climb in and out of, the Pivo was an ideal car for disabled drivers.

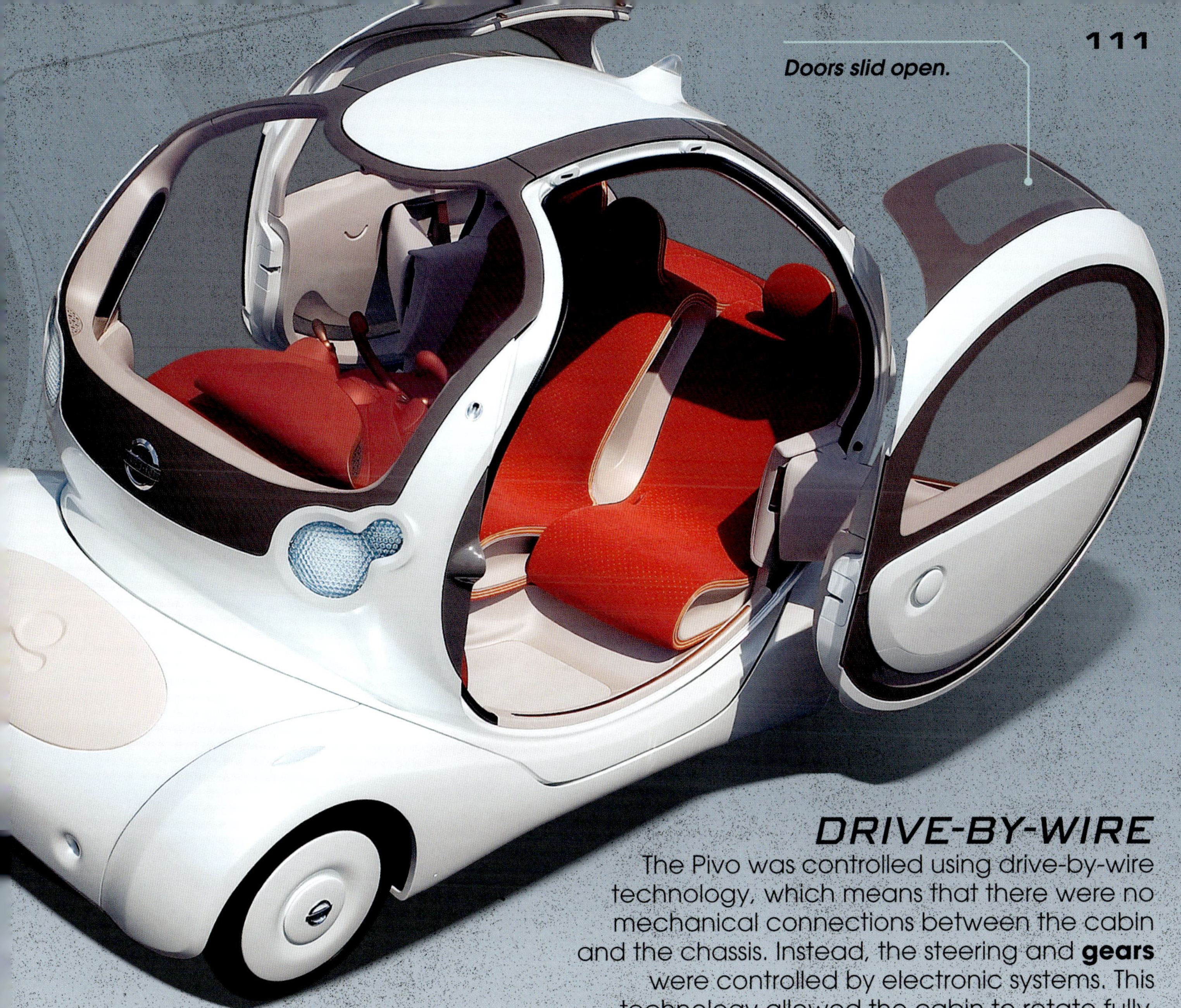

Doors slid open.

DRIVE-BY-WIRE

The Pivo was controlled using drive-by-wire technology, which means that there were no mechanical connections between the cabin and the chassis. Instead, the steering and **gears** were controlled by electronic systems. This technology allowed the cabin to rotate fully.

MASATO INOUE

As Chief Designer in Nissan's Exploratory Design Department, Masato Inoue is on a mission to build a **carbon-neutral** future. He develops stylish, affordable electric designs such as the Pivo, and hopes for a world in which every car on the road is like his creations, with no exhaust fumes and minimal noise pollution.

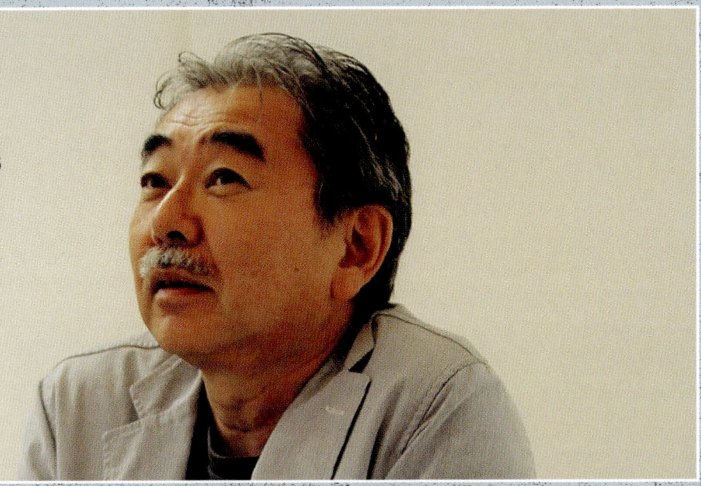

BMW

GINA

The shape-shifting GINA could change its form at will. It was covered in a thin 'skin' made from a durable, flexible fabric, stretched over a movable aluminium frame. This radical sports car was shown to the world in 2008 after seven years of secret development. It challenged our ideas about cars having a fixed shape.

SHIFTING FORM

The frame was moved by **hydraulic** controls, allowing the rear to raise up or lower and the headlamps to open and close (below). The fabric skin wrinkled up as the car shifted its form. The car could change shape in response to road and weather conditions. At high speeds, the rear spoiler grew to provide extra stability.

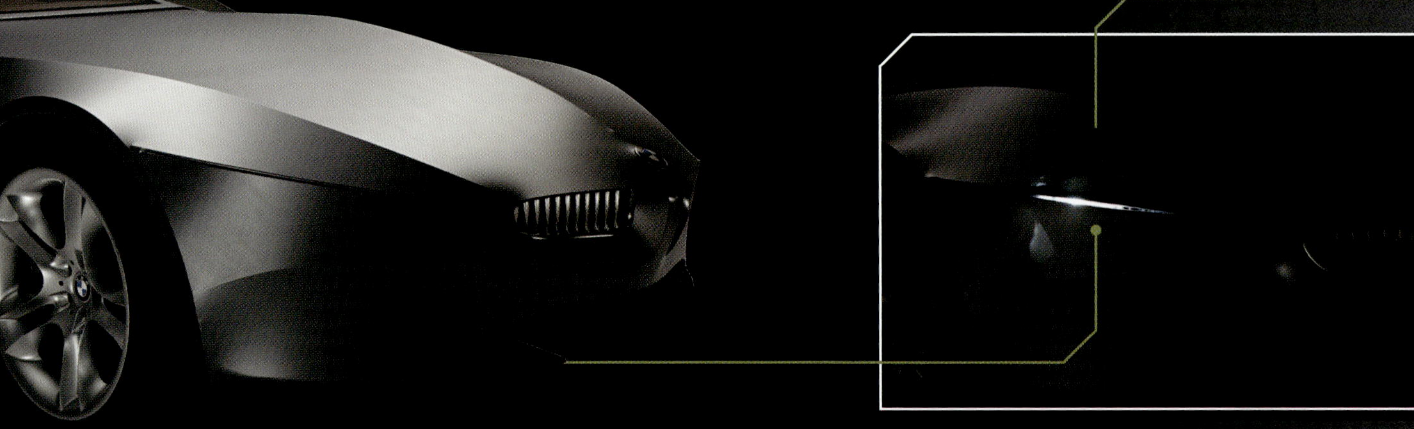

ENGINE ACCESS
The fabric covering was made from four separate panels: one covering the bonnet and the doors, another covering the boot, and one on either side. The front panel parted at the centre of the bonnet to allow access to the engine.

GINA

YEAR CREATED:
2008

ENGINE:
4.4 litre V8

TECH POINT

The fabric developed for the GINA was made using super-stretchy Lycra, a form of plastic used to make sportswear. It was water-resistant and durable. It was also able to resist very high or low temperatures and to expand and contract without damage. Fabric-covered cars have never hit the roads, but in 2016, BMW's new material was used to create Puma X-Cat trainers.

Fabric wrinkled when the doors were opened.

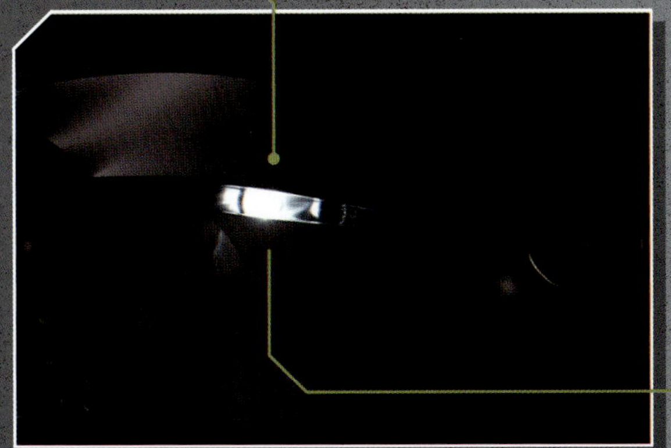

The fabric acted like eyelids over the headlights, blinking open when the lights were switched on.

EXALT

This saloon car was made using a range of innovative materials, including fibres made from volcanic rock. French manufacturer Peugeot wanted to show that it was possible to make a car without using oil-based materials.

OLD AND NEW

The Exalt mixed the new with the old. The steel bodywork was shaped by hand by a panel beater, a method used to make cars in the 1920s. However, the long bonnet, angled windscreen and low roof gave the car a sleek shape that was very much a 21st-century design.

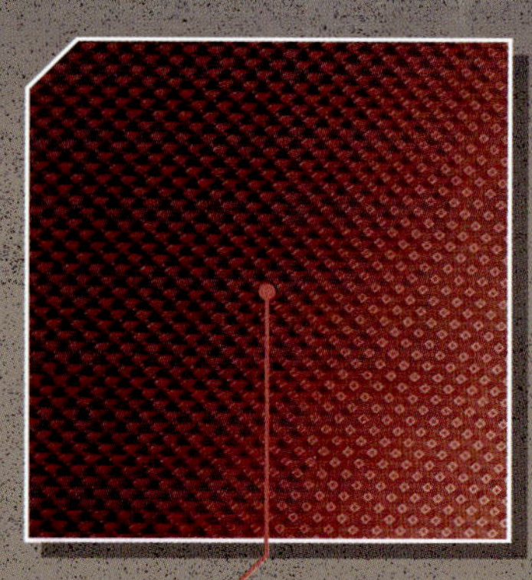

SLICK SKIN

The rear of the car was covered in artificial 'Shark Skin'. Its grainy structure mimicked a real shark's skin, and helped with the car's aerodynamics, allowing it to cut through the air.

EXALT

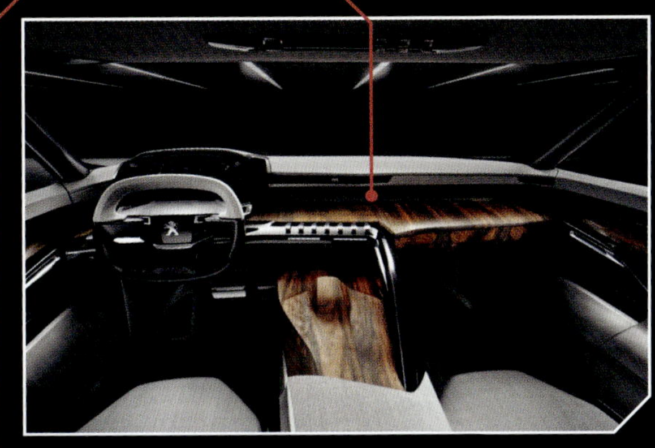

Underneath the natural materials was a high-tech control system. The dashboard featured nine toggle switches, to which the drivers could assign their own functions.

Sculpted bonnet reduced drag.

YEAR CREATED:
2014

WEIGHT:
1,700 kg

ENGINE:
Hybrid with a 1.6 litre petrol engine and a 50kW electric motor

POWER:
340 hp

LOCAL MATERIALS:
Peugeot proposed that they would vary the finish depending on the car's market. In the concept car, they used the wood ebony, chosen because it grows in Asia.

TECH POINT

The car's **sills** were made from basalt fibre. This is a material made from thin strands of basalt just a few millionths of a metre in diameter. Basalt is a rock produced by volcanic eruptions. To turn it into fibres, the rock is melted and passed through thin tubes. The resultant material is strong, light and fireproof.

The sills are underneath the doors.

PORSCHE

MISSION E

Unveiled in 2015, the Mission E was a statement by German manufacturer Porsche of their plans for a petrol-free future. An all-electric car, it went from concept to production in 2019, under the new name Taycan.

Car shape was similar to that of the 911, Porsche's most famous car.

ELECTRIC MOTORS

The Mission E was powered by two electric motors. One motor turned the front axle while the other turned the rear axle. Similar to the motors developed by Porsche for their racing car, the 919 Hybrid, they recovered energy during braking to make them more efficient. The motors were powered by a lithium-ion battery, which lay flat on the car's underbody, lowering its centre of gravity to give it better handling.

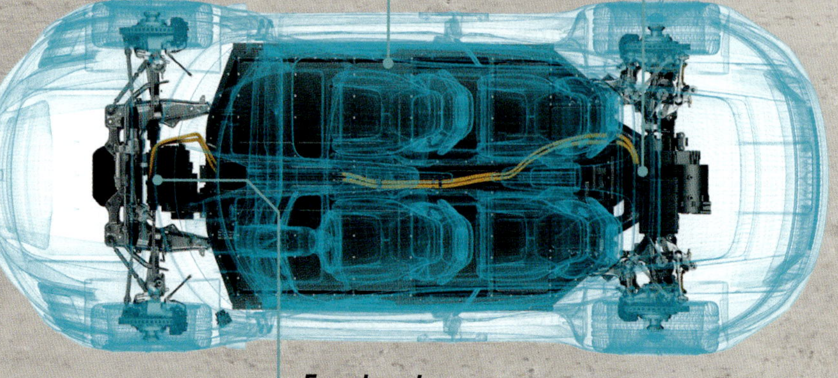

With a Turbo Charging system, the car's battery was charged to 80 per cent power in just 15 minutes. It could also be charged using technology called inductive charging. The car parked over a charger in the ground, and electricity passed through the air from a magnetic coil in the charger to a magnetic coil in the car.

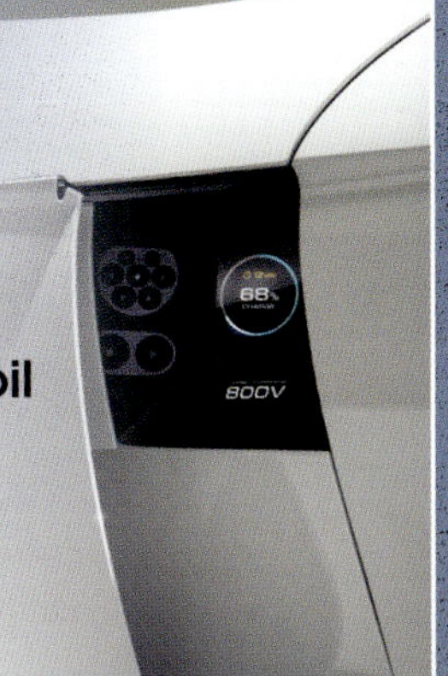

MISSION E

YEAR CREATED:
2015 (entered production in 2019)

WEIGHT:
2,140 kg

MOTOR:
800 V

POWER:
600 hp

0–100 KM/H:
3.5 seconds

0–200 KM/H:
12 seconds

TOP SPEED:
250 km/h

RANGE:
500 km

TIGHT CORNERING

The four wheels could all move independently from one another, and the amount of power transmitted to each wheel could be varied. When the car took a sharp corner, brake pressure slowed the inside rear wheel, and greater force was applied to the outside rear wheel. This made for sharp, sporty handling.

RENAULT
TREZOR

This slick electric sports car from French firm Renault was designed for speed. It was powered by a motor that was originally developed for the Formula E racing car.

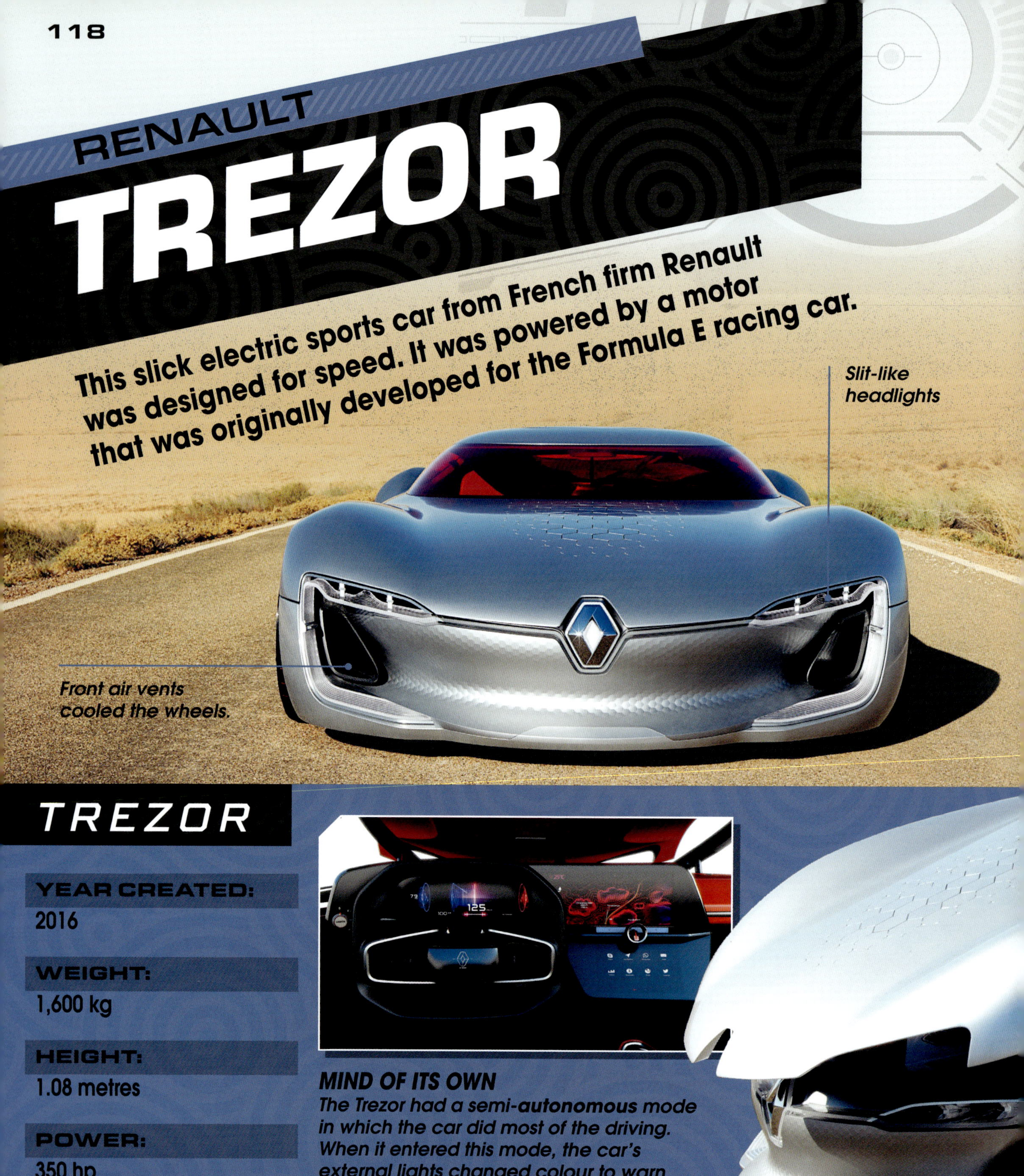

Slit-like headlights

Front air vents cooled the wheels.

TREZOR

YEAR CREATED:
2016

WEIGHT:
1,600 kg

HEIGHT:
1.08 metres

POWER:
350 hp

0–100 KM/H:
4 seconds

MIND OF ITS OWN
The Trezor had a semi-**autonomous** mode in which the car did most of the driving. When it entered this mode, the car's external lights changed colour to warn other drivers that the car was not being driven manually.

Air passed smoothly over the low roof.

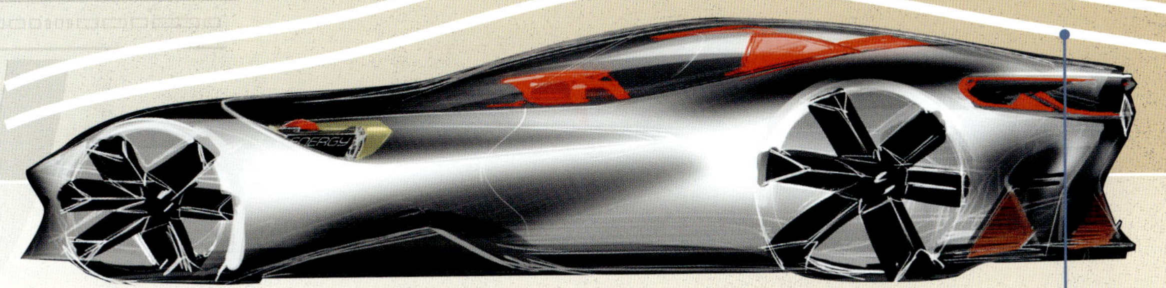

TECH POINT

The Trezor's sleek design made it one of the most aerodynamic cars in the world. A car's aerodynamics are measured by a number called a drag coefficient. Drag is caused by air resistance and is a force that slows down a moving object, working against the car's thrust, which powers it forwards. The lower the drag coefficient, the lower the drag. The Trezor had a drag coefficient of just 0.22. Most production cars are between 0.3 and 0.4.

RAISE THE ROOF

The car had no doors. Instead, the whole of the roof and bonnet raised up in a 'clamshell' opening. There were two seats for the driver and a passenger, and space for luggage in the front – dubbed a 'frunk'. Inside, the red leather and red wood matched the tinted visor-like windscreen.

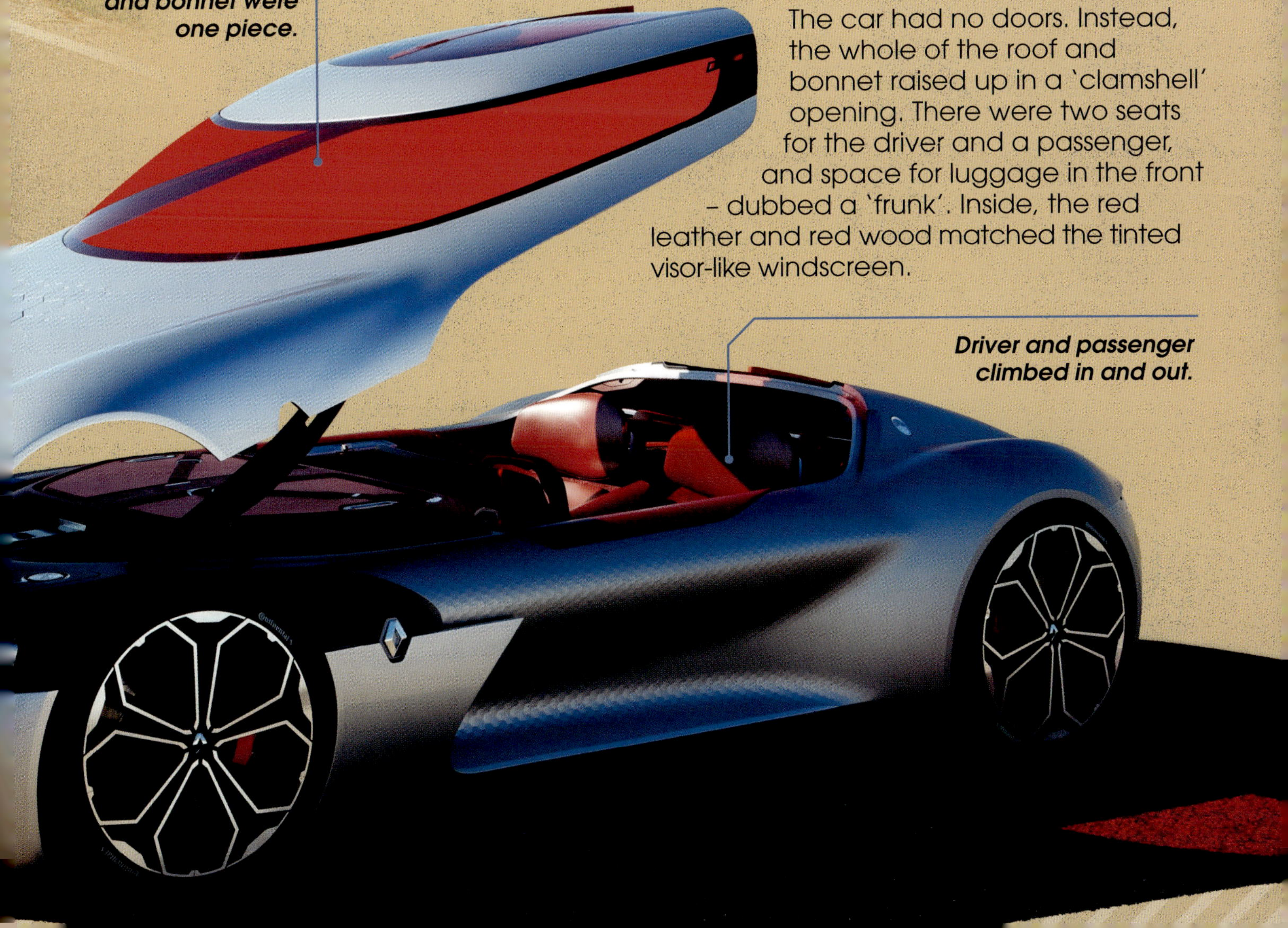

Roof, windscreen and bonnet were one piece.

Driver and passenger climbed in and out.

LAMBORGHINI
TERZO MILLENNIO

The Terzo Millennio was a glimpse of the supercar of the future. Lamborghini teamed up with scientists at Massachusetts Institute of Technology (MIT) to imagine how a fully electric supercar would work.

Wide front vents to cool motors and wheels.

SPEED TEST

To meet Lamborghini's performance standards, an electric vehicle needs to pass two simple tests. It has to have a top speed of more than 300 km/h, and it has to be capable of completing three laps at full speed around the Nürburgring race track in Germany. Together with the MIT scientists, Lamborghini's engineers are working on the new technology needed to pass this test.

The car's aerodynamics were tested in a wind tunnel.

TECH POINT

Lamborghini are developing supercapacitors to power the Terzo Millennio. These are capable of delivering more energy than normal lithium batteries, which would weigh the car down. Lamborghini are also exploring ways of storing energy by weaving billions of tiny copper wires into the body. This would turn the whole body into an energy-storage system, saving weight and improving performance.

SELF-REPAIRING CAR

Structural damage such as small cracks can be very dangerous in a speeding car. Inside the carbon-fibre body panels of the Terzo Millennio, sensors would detect any small cracks or dents. A computer would monitor the sensors and give instructions to tiny nanotubes in the panels that can repair themselves.

TERZO MILLENNIO

YEAR CREATED:

2017

TOP SPEED:

Over 300 km/h

VOLKSWAGEN
ID VIZZION

With no steering wheel or pedals, the ID Vizzion is a fully autonomous car that drives itself. German manufacturer Volkswagen hope to have an autonomous car for sale within the next few years, but driverless vehicles may still be a long way off.

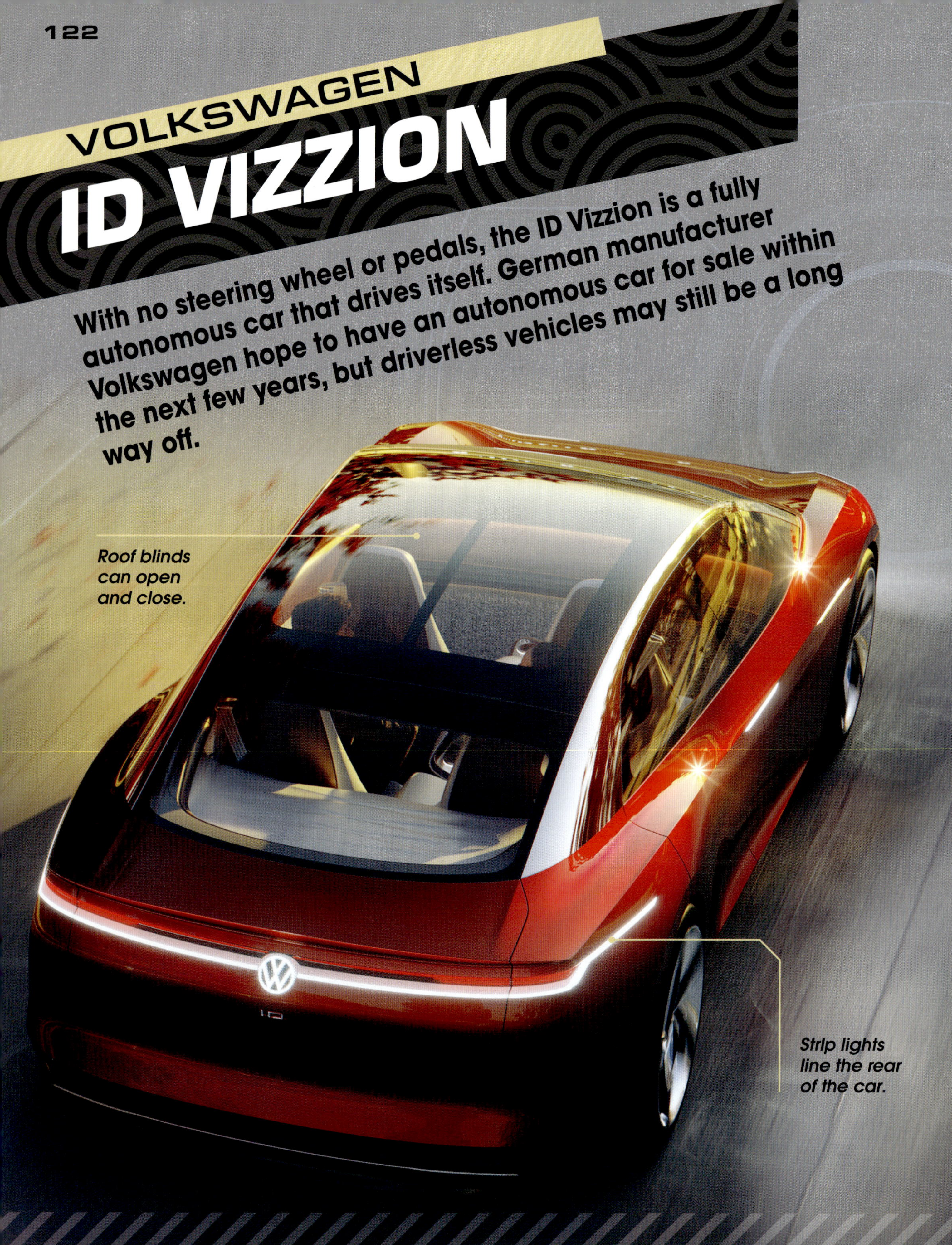

Roof blinds can open and close.

Strip lights line the rear of the car.

A virtual screen appears at the front of the car, showing travel information or even a movie.

ID VIZZION

YEAR CREATED:
2018

RANGE (ESTIMATE):
600 km

POWER:
Electric motor

VIRTUAL ASSISTANT

Passengers interact with the car via a three-dimensional **holographic** assistant called HoloLens. HoloLens is voice-activated, so there is no need to lift a finger. Tell the car that you need a coffee, and it will reroute itself to the nearest café for you. It will even monitor your temperature and heart rate to make sure you are comfortable.

TECH POINT

Sensors on the car monitor its surroundings using a system called LiDAR. The sensors send out pulses of laser light at up to 150,000 pulses per second. By measuring the time it takes for the pulses to bounce back, the LiDAR can calculate the distance between itself and objects around it and build up a map of its surroundings.

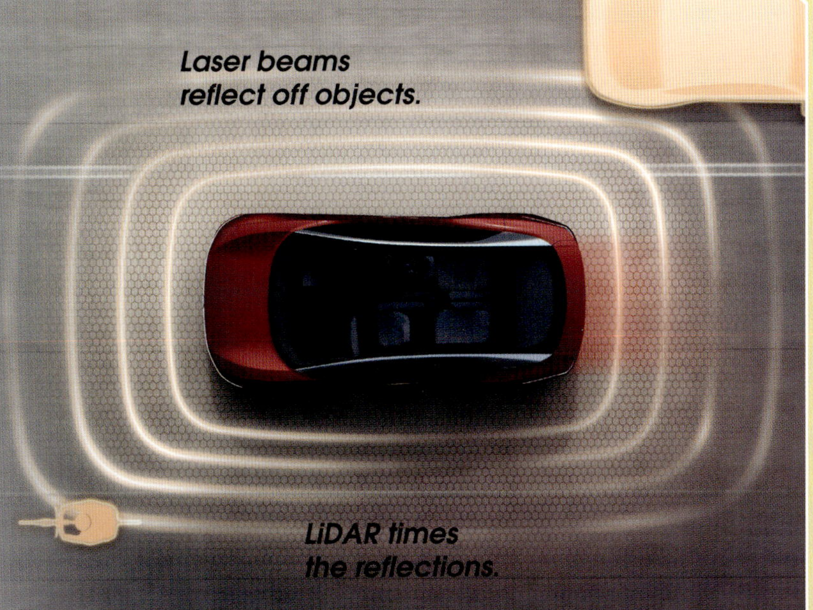

acceleration The rate at which a moving object's velocity is changing. The velocity of an object is its speed and direction of movement.

aerodynamics The way in which a gas or liquid moves around a solid object as it passes through it. Engineers study aerodynamics to produce cars with a shape that allows air to move around them smoothly.

alloy A material made by mixing two or more metals or by mixing metal with other substances.

automatic A car with a gearbox that changes gear automatically.

carbon fibre reinforced plastic (CFRP) A strong but lightweight material made from plastic with thin strands of carbon woven into it.

carbon-neutral Processes that add no extra carbon dioxide to the atmosphere. Carbon-neutral energy use helps to tackle global warming.

centre of gravity The point in an object around which its weight is balanced. Also called the centre of mass, it is the place from which the object's gravity acts.

chassis A strong frame to which the body of a car is attached.

chauffeur A professional driver employed to drive a private car.

clutch A mechanism in a car, normally operated by a pedal, that disconnects the engine from the gearbox to allow the driver to change gear.

coupé A car with a fixed roof and two doors.

cylinders The parts of an engine in which fuel is burned, pumping pistons to produce power.

disc brakes Brakes that slow a car down by clamping a pair of pads against a disc that is attached to each wheel.

downforce A force that pushes down on a car to keep it on the road. Parts of a racing car are designed to generate the right amount of downforce without slowing the car down too much.

drag A force that resists the movement of an object through a gas or liquid. Drag acts in the opposite direction to the direction of the movement, slowing the object down.

endurance race A motor race in which cars drive as far as they can within a fixed amount of time.

gearbox The system of gears in a car. Gears change the speed at which the engine's power drives the wheels.

gears A series of interlocking cogs connecting a car's engine to its wheels.

greenhouse gas A gas that contributes to global warming if it is released into the atmosphere.

handling The ease with which a driver can control a car.

holographic Made of holograms – two-dimensional images that appear to be three-dimensional.

horsepower (hp) A unit of measurement for power, or the rate at which work is done. One horsepower is roughly equal to the power of one strong horse.

hybrid A car that is powered by a combination of a petrol engine and one or more electric motors.

hydraulics A power system in which fluids are used to transfer force from one place to another.

LED Short for Light-Emitting Diode. A device that gives off light when electricity is passed through it.

manual A car with a gearbox that is controlled by the driver.

monocoque A strong exterior shell to a vehicle that provides it with structural support.

muscle car A powerful road car with a large engine.

navigation Planning a route from where you are now to the place you wish to get to. Modern cars have computerised navigation systems that monitor the car's location using satellite technology.

Newton metre A unit of measurement for turning force.

prototype A model of a new design that is made to test out the design.

roll cage A strong metal frame that protects the driver in the event of a crash.

running boards Platforms fitted to the sides of old cars to help people to climb in.

sills The parts of a car that run along the side underneath the doors. The sills are strong supporting parts in the structure of a car.

spoiler A part on a car designed to create downforce by increasing drag.

stock car An ordinary road car that has been strengthened for racing.

suspension A system of springs and shock absorbers that attach the wheels to a car's chassis.

transmission The part of a car that transfers power from the engine to the wheels via a gearbox.

turbine A machine with blades that spin when a gas or liquid is passed through them. Turbines are used in gas turbine engines to provide a constant supply of power.

turbocharger A device, powered by the exhaust, that increases the pressure of the air that is fed into an engine's cylinders. This helps the fuel to burn, increasing the power of the engine.

INDEX

A

B

C

D

E

F

G

First published in Great Britain
in 2026 by Wayland
Copyright © Hodder and Stoughton Limited, 2026
All rights reserved
The material in this book has previously appeared
in the *Motormania* series by Rob Colson

Based on books produced by Tall Tree Ltd
Interior pages designer: Jonathan Vipond
Cover designer: Peter Scoulding

HB ISBN: 978 1 5263 3254 7
PB ISBN: 978 1 5263 3246 2
Ebook ISBN: 978 1 5263 3247 9

Wayland
An imprint of Hachette Children's Group
Part of Hodder and Stoughton Limited
Carmelite House
50 Victoria Embankment
London EC4Y 0DZ

An Hachette UK Company
www.hachette.co.uk
www.hachettechildrens.co.uk

Printed and bound in China

The authorised representative in the EEA is Hachette
Ireland, 8 Castlecourt Centre, Dublin 15, D15 XTP3, Ireland
(email: info@hbgi.ie)